Guided by Grace

The Kathleen Mallory Story

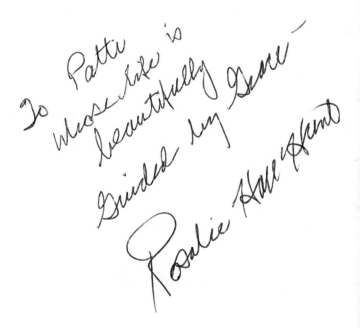

To Patti
whose life is
beautifully
Guided by Grace ~

Rosalie Hall Hunt

ROSALIE HALL HUNT

Guided by Grace: The Kathleen Mallory Story

Copyright 2020 Rosalie Hall Hunt

All Rights Reserved

ISBN: 978-1-940645-85-8

Greenville, South Carolina

PUBLISHED IN THE UNITED STATES OF AMERICA

ENDORSEMENTS

From the day I came to WMU headquarters in 2002, I heard the name "Kathleen Mallory." I began researching her life and was soon overwhelmed by her impact on WMU, the Southern Baptist Convention and the world of missions. She was called a "quiet force," and the "sweetheart of Southern Baptists." I have been privileged to know every national WMU executive director since Mallory's tenure. But, oh, how I wish I could have met her as well. Through the heart and words of Rosalie Hunt, I now get to meet her!

— David George, President
Woman's Missionary Union Foundation, SBC

Kathleen Moore Mallory, a uniquely gifted woman who led Woman's Missionary Union through two world wars and the Great Depression. She was known among leaders of the Southern Baptist Convention as the "Tiny Dynamo." A dynamo leader, because of a devoted prayer life, that was life-changing for those praying along with her. Come on a journey with gifted author Rosalie Hunt as she navigates us into the heart and mind of Kathleen Mallory, a genuinely humble servant of the Lord. Her story is brought to life by one uniquely gifted woman writing about another.

— Linda Cooper, President
National Woman's Missionary Union

Rosalie Hunt has helped us rediscover Kathleen Mallory, the "tiny dynamo," as she was known in her many years of leadership. It is no overstatement to see Mallory as one of the "giants of the faith." Hunt has made it possible for Southern Baptists, and for all who love missions, to explore in depth the life of this missions hero. Read it and hear the voice of Kathleen Mallory as it continues to reverberate into this new millennium.

— *Rick Lance, Executive Director*
Alabama Baptist State Board of Missions

In this captivating book, WMU mission historian and author Rosalie Hunt takes you on the life journey of Kathleen Mallory, God's fruit-bearing servant leader. Bearing fruit that remains is the evidence of a life well-lived and is the desire of every woman surrendered to God and His mission. As you read, you will see how Mallory's service to Christ impacted her generation and launched His mission cause for future generations. And you will be inspired to reflect on your *own* life journey, asking yourself, "Will my life produce fruit that remains?"

— *Cindy Townsend, Director, Women's Ministries, WMU,*
First Baptist Church Jackson, Mississippi;
Former Executive Director,
Louisiana WMU and Mississippi WMU

Just as she gave us meticulous insights into the lives of Ann Judson, Hephzibah Jenkins Townsend, and Fannie Heck, Rosalie Hall Hunt has captured the life of our beloved Kathleen Mallory. Hunt's new book emphatically demonstrates that the dreams in a little girl's heart have no limitations. At the age of ten, Kathleen gave her heart to Jesus. She credited her dear home church with giving her the foundational discipline for her Christian faith. Kathleen's charm, intelligence and personality prepared her to change the shape and reach of Woman's Missionary Union for the next century. I encourage you to do more than simply read her story — implement her prayer life and faith in God.

— Anna Speir, WMU Director, First Baptist Church,
Selma, Alabama (Kathleen Mallory's home church)
and Former President, Alabama WMU

As a lifelong Alabama Baptist, I've often heard about the strategic role of the famous missions leader from our state, Kathleen Mallory, but it took the work of Rosalie Hunt, in her new book, to help me truly know Miss Mallory. Hunt's unique style of transporting the reader into the same moment, same conversation and same experience as Miss Mallory allows us to gain a glimpse of her gracious heart and skillful mind while also grasping the tremendous influence she had on Southern Baptist missions, then and now. Maintaining strength and poise under pressure, resilient, willing to serve others before herself, disciplined, firm but gentle — traits we could all learn to enhance in our own lives. Hunt helps us walk in the steps of a legend who achieved all of these and more. So, whether you are interested in missions history, leadership development or spiritual formation, this book is well worth your time.

— Jennifer Davis Rash
President and Editor-in-Chief
TAB Media/The Alabama Baptist

When I think of Kathleen Mallory, I am reminded of the Apostle Paul when he challenges us to be imitators of God. Such is the life of Kathleen Mallory, the longest-tenured leader of Woman's Missionary Union. Gentle, humble, and a woman of prayer, she led in one of the greatest missions discipleship movements of our time, moving Southern Baptists forward for the cause of the Great Commission. A life well-lived and a story so beautifully told through author Rosalie Hunt.

— *Candace McIntosh, Executive Director*
Alabama Woman's Missionary Union

DEDICATION

To Anna Speir and the remarkable
WMU women of First Baptist Church,
Selma, Alabama — Kathleen Mallory's home church

TABLE OF CONTENTS

FOREWORD

Delighted was I to learn Kathleen Mallory accepted a radio as a gift from her nieces and nephews to indulge in light diversions of listening to classical music. Consider for a moment the life span of Woman's Missionary Union as a symphony. As in most orchestra concerts, the opening movement is loud and lively, rambunctious and vigorous. Such was the case with the creation of the Union. There were alternating solos between two commanding performers — Annie Armstrong and Fannie E.S. Heck.

The leadership of Kathleen Mallory could be considered the second major movement of the orchestra symphony. The awe-inspiring *fortissimo* dynamic of the opening has subsided, and now we settle into the rhythmic and lyrical pace that keeps eager listeners engaged. In this particular movement, there are no soloists. It is absolutely understood the piece is under the full control of God as conductor. The concertmaster, Kathleen Mallory, does her best to draw from the most reserved and reticent musicians incredibly rich sounds that reverberate for all eternity. The heterophony that was created, which layered in harmonious voices using the same main melody of missions, is breathtakingly beautiful.

You will be so glad you purchased a ticket and experienced the concert. Rosalie Hunt is masterful at communicating this musical genre. You will be on the edge of your front-row, center-section seat for the entire performance, feeling the vibration each time the timpani are struck with a mallet. As the *ritardando* and *diminuendo* engage, and the tempo and volume gradually decrease, your entire focus will be captivated long after the music has ended. Sit back and enjoy the longest symphonic movement in the entire history of Woman's Missionary Union.

— *Sandy Wisdom-Martin, Executive Director-Treasurer*
Woman's Missionary Union, SBC

PREFACE

Unique. Unparalleled. It requires a pantheon of adjectives to describe Kathleen Mallory, the gifted woman who led Woman's Missionary Union for a remarkable thirty-six years. Lovely, graceful, charming, the epitome of Southern graciousness, yet it was the depth of her *spiritual* gifts that influenced a generation of women, and, indeed, the entire Southern Baptist Convention. Deceptively dainty, never pushy, yet amazingly resilient, she led WMU through two world wars and the Great Depression. Kathleen Moore Mallory, with her incisive skill and tenacity, led women to rescue the denomination's two mission boards from crushing debt. Over a period of more than three decades, Mallory came to be known among leaders of the Southern Baptist Convention as the "Tiny Dynamo."

Kathleen lost the love of her life to tuberculosis the spring before their scheduled wedding date. Then, a China missionary's letter fell like a spark into the tinder of her heart, and God redirected her path to missions service through magnificently leading the women of WMU in kingdom service. Among her many unique characteristics was Kathleen Mallory's incredible self-discipline. There has never been another one to equal her in WMU's history. She always declared she was "too bossy to be a teacher," but she gently bossed the world's largest missions organization for women with a deceptively gentle hand. The secret to her incredible success? Prayer. The renowned Alma Hunt, who followed her as executive director, stated that the reason for Kathleen Mallory's remarkable strength and poise under pressure was rooted in her prayer life. It was absolutely unique and left a lasting impression on all who had the privilege of hearing her pray and praying along with her. It was life-changing.

Kathleen Mallory's life of service as WMU's executive director began at the tender age of thirty-three. She grew up as a daughter of privilege but lived most frugally, giving most of her money to missions. Mallory never owned a car or a house, always living in a tiny apartment. Yet, she traveled widely and wrote prolifically. One of the secrets of her strong leadership lay in her ability to unbendingly stand for her convictions — but when the majority voted differently, she gracefully threw her weight behind that opinion. By the time of her retirement at sixty-nine, she held a position of high esteem in the entire convention.

Capturing the essence of Kathleen Mallory's remarkable life is made difficult by the dearth of personal material she left. Although she wrote extensively about missions, she wrote no autobiography, purposely saved very few personal letters — maybe half a dozen — kept no journal, and did not maintain a diary. However, in the hundreds of business letters she left, a key to her personality is reflected in her unique sentence structure. In reading the many letters written by Kathleen Mallory, I realized that not once did she begin a sentence with the pronoun "I." This is quite a commentary on the character of a remarkably talented and brilliant woman, one who was in a position of distinct authority for a woman in the early twentieth century, but was, nonetheless, genuinely humble. She *lived* the essence of the passage in Philippians 2:3: "In lowliness of mind let each esteem others better than himself" (New King James Version). This account of Baptists' tiny dynamo, Kathleen Mallory, is a journey into the heart and mind of a uniquely gifted woman of God.

ACKNOWLEDGMENTS

This account of the life of Kathleen Moore Mallory is not historical fiction. It is narrative based on fact. The conversations contained herein are based on my understanding of Kathleen's words and conversational style developed from the countless business letters she wrote while serving as executive director of WMU for thirty-six years. She saved scarcely any personal letters. Some conversations are direct quotes, as recorded by a close friend, Annie Wright Ussery, who knew Kathleen Mallory from childhood. Kathleen, a close friend of Annie's mother, Alma (Mrs. Carter) Wright, was frequently in their home, and Ussery wrote a brilliant account of Mallory's life and ministry shortly after Kathleen's death in 1954. A huge debt of gratitude goes to Mrs. Ussery for capturing the spirit and essence of Kathleen Mallory and making it available to us. Had she not recorded key incidents in Mallory's life, including her personal memories, they would have been lost to history.

I first became interested in Kathleen Mallory when hearing about her as a small child living in China. Because of Kathleen Mallory and WMU, my mother's salary for the first five years she served as a Southern Baptist missionary in China was provided by Woman's Missionary Union. I joined the WMU fan club as a little MK (missionaries' kid) and have maintained my membership!

There is another whose contributions to the life and legacy of Kathleen Mallory are incalculable. Catherine Allen captured Mallory's essence in *Laborers Together with God*. All through the documentation on Kathleen found in the archives of WMU in Birmingham are records placed there by Catherine Allen, resulting from her research for the book. Allen is personally a treasure trove of WMU history, a leading authority on Baptist women in missions. Cindy Goodwin, retired WMU leader living in Birmingham and volunteer archivist, has been of tremendous assistance in locating materials in the WMU archives. Those archives are the main repository for the record of Mallory's life and contributions.

Archivists are indispensable, and Taffey Hall of the Southern Baptist Historical Library and Archives in Nashville has been an outstanding source of Mallory history, providing hundreds of letters of Mallory correspondence with Una Roberts Lawrence, Nannie Helen Burroughs, and Dr. W.O. Carver. Fascinating bits of information and personal insight into the heart and mind of Kathleen Mallory were discovered in those letters.

Cindy Johnson, retired WMU archivist, was another source of help. Highly knowledgeable about Mallory, and having worked with WMU archives for many years, Johnson led the way to several key sources. Kyndal Owens, archivist at the International Mission Board (formerly Foreign Mission Board), was key in gathering information about correspondence between Mallory and the various FMB presidents who served during her tenure.

Personal touches came from people still living who knew Kathleen when they were young, or had personal family knowledge of her. Their blended voices added authenticity to the traits that history has said belonged to Kathleen Mallory. June Whitlow, longtime executive at national WMU, vividly remembers when, as a teenager, she saw Miss Mallory, dressed in a lovely blue dress, speaking at a gathering. Mary Jo Drake Maples of Guntersville,

Alabama, recalled meeting her when she was young. Kathleen was a personal friend of Maples' mother, Hilda Hall Drake, an Alabama WMU leader, and Mary Jo retains a vivid memory of the gentle loveliness of Miss Mallory. Another, Joyce Rogers, recalls meeting Miss Mallory for the first and only time when the Mallory Center was dedicated in Baltimore in 1953. That center changed a young girl's life forever. Angie Cooper, longtime Kathleen Mallory fan in Alabama, told of stories recounted to her from a number of women who knew Mallory personally and who had the privilege of volunteering at national headquarters and serving briefly with the legendary leader.

Candy Patterson, WMU leader in Guntersville, Alabama, volunteered on numerous occasions to travel with me to do research in archives and to visit "Kathleen spots" in Selma. Candy is a treasure. The peerless assistance of Anna Speir, state WMU leader and longtime WMU member and leader in Kathleen's own First Baptist Church, Selma, WMU, made countless family contacts and site visits in Selma and surrounding areas possible. Anna is also a link with Kathleen's past, for Kathleen Mallory's beloved niece Jacqueline was an active and elderly member of the WMU group Anna joined over forty years ago. Jacqueline would have done her aunt proud in her zeal and enthusiasm for mission service. Anna also traveled with me and introduced me to a number of Kathleen's great nieces and nephews. Mallory and Martha Reeves, Edgar Reeves, Sue Privett Whatley, and Martha Reeves Crosland were instrumental in providing family pictures and stories, some in family lore, and some from their personal memories of their cherished "Artie." Both the cover and the editing and preparing of pictures for this volume are the work of Eric Hudiburg, photographer based in Raleigh, North Carolina, and, incidentally, our grandson.

Also gifted is one who makes Kathleen's story readable: Ella Robinson, longtime editor for WMU, now retired — but, thankfully for me, *not* completely retired and here to help tell the story. And so much of what we do in WMU and missions service in this new millennium is thanks to the one who went before us and lighted the path: Kathleen Moore Mallory.

Guided by Grace

The Kathleen Mallory Story

Summerfield, Alabama: The house where Kathleen Mallory was born, circa 1830

CHAPTER ONE

1879

*L*ate-night embers gently glowed in the fireplace as Louisa Mallory dreamily watched their flickering lights. Winters in Alabama were usually not severe, but fires helped to cut the chill that invaded the house in early January. "Hugh," she whispered softly, "are you still awake?" At the sound of his wife's voice, Hugh was instantly alert. "Luta, is it time? Baby's coming?" His voice sounded anxious. Louisa smiled at his use of her childhood nickname, and she quickly reassured him, "No, no, but I can tell

— it won't be long. That's what comes from having two little ones already." He asked, "Are you hurting, my dear? Shall I get you a warm drink?" Reaching over to pat his arm, Louisa responded, "Thoughtful as always, dear Hugh. No, I'm just lying here trying to think of a name for our baby. Do you have a favorite?"

Hugh chuckled, "Thinking of names at midnight? Don't you mean two names? We don't know if we're having a boy or a girl." Louisa mused, "Well, our five-year-old has your name and Maria Louisa has part of mine, so now maybe we should branch out a bit." Hugh picked up the challenge, responding, "You pick one for a daughter and I'll choose for a son." Then, thoughtfully, he reached for her hand, "Luta, I'd love to name a boy James, for my father. I just wish Dad was still living. He has been gone well over a year now, but I still miss him," Hugh sighed. Louisa patted his arm comfortingly, "I know he would be so pleased to have a little namesake. And if baby is a girl," she continued, "I'd like to name her Kathleen. It has always seemed like a beautiful name to me. Then," she paused as she thought it over, "maybe the middle name for my family — Moore." Hugh chuckled, "Now let's get to sleep so baby James — or Kathleen — can rest. And so can we."

Louisa was slow to drop off to sleep as she lay thinking about the weeks ahead, increasingly thankful that her father was a doctor and had brought many little ones into the world. The sleepy little village of Summerfield, Louisa's childhood home, was just about eight miles away. Her father, Clement Moore, was the town's leading physician. She and Hugh had exchanged their wedding vows in front of the mantel in the Moores' parlor. That old house, on the corner of Centenary and Main Street, held many memories for her, and she loved the fact that each of her children had been born there. She and Hugh had set up housekeeping in nearby Selma, where his law practice flourished. An historic little city on the Alabama River, Selma was a center for trade and commerce and had been a strategic location in the recent and devastating war between the states. Louisa vividly remembered the privations and horrors of war — practically on their doorstep — and prayed that their children would never have to face such devastation and turmoil.

At the moment, this baby's safe arrival into the world was their primary concern. Dr. Moore had delivered both Hugh Jr. and Maria Louisa in Summerfield just a few years earlier, and Louisa herself had first seen the light of day in the Moore house. Louisa drifted to sleep on the thought that in just a matter of days she needed to head toward Summerfield and not chance going into labor away from her father and medical help.

Early on the crisp Monday morning of January 20, Louisa gave her two little ones long hugs and promised to bring them a big surprise from Grandmama and Granddaddy's house. The children's nurse, Nellie, beamed as she stood with the little ones, an arm around each. "Now don't you worry, Miz Louisa, these babies are going to be fine while you are away." Young Hugh looked indignant, "But, Nellie, I am not a baby!" he spoke with the assurance of a sturdy five-year-old. Nellie hastily agreed and peace was restored.

As the horses carefully picked their way down the rutted road, Hugh was anxious about Louisa's condition. Winter conditions made the hard-packed dirt of the road bumpy. "Not to worry," she assured her husband, "I don't feel pains yet, but I'm thinking it won't be many more days." Returning to her childhood home was always a comforting feeling, and Dr. Moore knew just how to calm the nerves of an expectant mother. He was a favorite with young mothers all over the district. Many a time he had been asked the question: "Oh, Dr. Moore! Are you the Clement Moore who wrote 'Twas the Night Before Christmas?" "Alas," he would respond, "I'm afraid poetry isn't in my line, but I do like to conclude my doctor's calls with the same greeting that Clement Moore used with his Christmas tale — 'and to you a good night!'" Dr. Moore's kind face and twinkling eyes often made his patients think of the jolly old man in their favorite holiday poem.

Jacqueline Louisa Moore met her daughter at the door with a big hug, leading her immediately toward the crackling fire in the cheerful parlor. "A cup of warm chocolate is just what the doctor ordered," she assured the expectant parents with a twinkle in her eyes. "We are excited about this blessed event!" Mallory soon headed back to Selma but promised to return in a few days, determined to be there when Louisa's time came.

For several days, Louisa reveled in the pleasure of being home with her parents and shamelessly enjoyed her mother's coddling of her "Luta." Since Louisa was named for her mother, the family had always distinguished between the two by calling her Luta. Come Thursday afternoon, she was relieved to see Hugh drive up, and, as if on schedule, Luta went into labor that night. Having her father, with his gentle hands and reassuring voice, care for her helped make the pain bearable, but the night seemed to last forever. Through a haze of pain, Louisa could hear voices, but her mind could only measure the level of pain each moment held. And then, the voices faded away and she fell into an exhausted sleep. Louisa slowly roused to find Hugh bending over her, cradling their newborn, swathed in one of Jacqueline Moore's soft, knit receiving blankets. "Luta," Hugh beamed, "wake up and meet our baby." Louisa's eyes lighted, "Hugh," she gave a tired smile, "am I meeting James or Kathleen?" Her husband chuckled, "You are the one who picked this babe's name, my dear. Meet our beautiful little Kathleen."

Louisa's heart swelled with tenderness as she took the tiny infant and carefully turned back the corners of the blanket. Wondering blue eyes stared back at her in the unfocused look of all newborns. It was love at first sight, and the new mother breathed, "Oh, Hugh, have you ever seen such beautiful blue eyes before?" As she reached out a finger to caress the tiny cheek, the baby's head seemed to turn instinctively in the direction of her mother's touch, and Louisa's heart melted. Dr. Moore bustled in about this time to compliment his daughter on her perseverance and bravery. "Father," Louisa spoke softly, "you have delivered a 'Kathleen' tonight." She smiled as she added, "And her full name is to be Kathleen Moore Mallory." Clement Moore beamed with pleasure, and tears welled a bit in his eyes at the signal honor.

As soon as Dr. Moore felt it safe for daughter and grandchild to travel, tiny Kathleen was carefully bundled up and on her way to Selma, which would be her home until adulthood and to which she would one day return to spend her final quiet years. At the moment, the proud parents were concentrating on this new addition to the family and discussing, as new parents often tend to do, just what might the future look like for this perfect little child. Louisa was grateful that her parents lived nearby and could be part of their children's lives. At the same time, she felt a bit guilty, because Anne Marie, Kathleen's other grandmother, lived some 100 miles away in Talladega County. Traveling such a distance was no simple task. Both of the Mallorys regretted even more that this little one would never be able to know her grandfather James Mallory. He had died late in 1877, and not a day passed that Hugh did not think of something he wished he could discuss with Father. He remembered how proudly James and Anne Marie Mallory had introduced their beautiful new daughter-in-law to all their relatives and to their Alpine Baptist Church family in 1872 when he and Louisa had made a wedding trip there just after their marriage. Hugh had been born and grew up on the family's small plantation called Selwood, and he had a storehouse of happy childhood memories. He was determined to regularly share family tales with this little one and her siblings as they grew up so the children could appreciate both sides of the family.

Louisa's mother had prepared hot bricks to keep their feet warm on the buggy ride home, and Louisa made sure no cold January air endangered the baby. Hugh seemed to be in a contemplative mood as they made the journey. "Luta," he sighed, "this babe is born into a much different world than did we some thirty years ago. Just think," and he paused, "back then we lived in a thriving land and had no notion that war lay ahead of us and would change the way in which our ancestors had lived for years." Louisa broke in, "But, Hugh, we are more fortunate than so many. You lost none of your brothers who fought in the war, and you, young though you were, survived the skirmishes in which you were involved. And so young you were! And," she concluded, "it's up to us to be sure our Kathleen learns to know and love God and be thankful for His blessings." Mallory paused and then reached over to kiss her cheek, "That is surely our goal with all of our dear children, Luta. We will not fail." Then he added on a tender note, "This baby will be blessed with the best of mothers; that I know for a fact."

As the buggy drew near the large Victorian house on Lapsley Street, Mallory's thoughts returned to the present moment. Looking over into the sweetly sleeping face of their little Kathleen, he wondered aloud, "Luta, how do you think big brother and sister are going to feel about a new baby in the family? Guess there is going to be some jealousy?" Louisa smiled serenely, "I really have no fears, dear Hugh. They are going to think this is their newest play-pretty. They'll probably fight over who gets to hold her the most." And her prophecy quickly came true as they reached the house, only to find two little ones jumping up and down in excitement, Nellie standing with them, admonishing each to calm down and see their new surprise. Little Louisa (called "Louise" to distinguish her from her mother) was on tiptoe to peek into the blanket and exclaim over the sight of a tiny, wiggling baby, who, as if on cue, opened her beautiful blue eyes and gave a little baby sound, somewhere between a sigh and a coo. Big brother Hugh and sister Louisa were instantly smitten, willing slaves to this live doll. Hugh and Louisa enfolded their brood in their arms, and gave thanks for manifold blessings.

Kathleen at three

CHAPTER TWO

1882-1889

*L*azy Sunday afternoons in the big room the Mallory children called the nursery were some of Kathleen's earliest memories. The chubby-cheeked little sprite remembered forever the crackling of the friendly fire kept burning to ward off winter chills, windows closed to the gentle sound of rain and listening to Mother read wonderful storybooks. Sometimes brother Hugh would take a turn reading; Kathleen adored Hugh. He was five years older and spoiled her dreadfully. Sister Maria Louisa ("Louise"), only three years older than Kathleen, was happily under her little sister's chubby thumb and willing to let Kathleen make the decisions, a role that suited that nimble-witted toddler to perfection.

Louisa Mallory was an astute reader of character, especially that of her growing brood of children. She had been one of several children herself and knew firsthand about give-and-take. She loved watching the interactions of these young ones of hers. Hugh Jr. enjoyed being big brother and was a bit superior in knowledge and experience. Nonetheless, he was putty in Kathleen's hands. Louise, who was on the move much of the time, was next in age and particularly relished dancing. It was their sister Kathleen, looking younger than her age and with a mind as agile as her feet, however, who kept things lively. As the years passed and personality traits became increasingly pronounced, their mother loved telling family and friends who commented on Kathleen's engaging sweet nature, "Why, anyone can get along with Kathleen as long as they do things her way!"

Nellie, their household help and nurse to the young ones, loved all the children and often indulged them. She frequently commented that Kathleen was "too sweet to spoil." Nellie was a constant in the lives of all the children. Baby Bessie came along when Kathleen was three, and Louisa's wise handling of all her children managed to prevent jealousy from developing. Kathleen and her siblings all looked up to their lovely and perceptive mother. Louisa was known both at home and in their church for being calm and quiet, never flashy, yet always steady and strong in character. In later years, Kathleen could look back and recognize that her mother made a habit of looking for ways to encourage others. Clearly, the manner in which Louisa and Hugh Mallory involved their children in working together to make family decisions influenced the way Kathleen would later know how to graciously deal with issues where *her* choice was not always the majority choice. Kathleen did indeed love to get her way, but she learned early how to accept majority rule and then wholeheartedly support whatever decision had been made, even if it differed from her own.

Hugh Mallory was affectionately known as "Col'nel Mallory" or simply, "The Colonel" in Selma, and his rapidly expanding law practice reflected the goodwill in which he was held by all who knew him. Tiny Kathleen adored her father. Hugh Mallory was not an especially tall man, but in the eyes of his adoring daughter he was forever a giant. Busy as his law practice was, Hugh always managed to find time for his children. Kathleen, mentally sharp and intuitively observant, found in him a beautiful pattern of fatherhood. That, in turn, made it exceptionally easy for her to view God as a loving Heavenly Father. Hugh invariably took time to lead the family in devotions each morning, and this practice became a lifetime habit for Kathleen.

Trips to Summerfield and Grandmother and Grandfather were always high points of excitement. Grandmother Moore spoiled her dreadfully, and Kathleen loved every moment of it. Mother tended to be more strict and expect a lot of her, but, with Grandmother, she could revel in indulgent attention. Grandmother Moore told lovely family stories of long-ago days, stories of their ancestors in Virginia, telling of the well-known Byrd and King families and the lovely plantation homes her own mother used to describe. Just as special to Kathleen was Granddaddy Moore and his fascinating black medicine bag, worn from much use, and filled with an intriguing supply of salves and powders. She eyed with a delicious shudder the knives he assured her that he only used "when absolutely necessary." Kathleen considered her beloved grandfather a hero, always picking up that black bag and heading off to help someone who was desperately ill or bringing a new baby into the world. Grandfather could spin a fine yarn and loved to laugh with his grandchildren as he told them tales of his own boyhood in Georgia.

Kathleen never forgot a night late one August when Grandfather Moore came knocking on their door in Selma, ordering each of his grandchildren to get up right then and go the eight miles to Summerfield with him. Yellow fever had broken out and was always more dangerous in the city, especially one in the lowlands. Summerfield was a bit higher in elevation and had the advantage of being more isolated. It would afford his grandchildren more safety. The memory of that midnight ride through the countryside remained permanently in Kathleen's mind.

Kathleen loved to explore Selma, especially when big brother Hugh could take them around in the carriage. With her dark blonde curls and bright blue eyes, Kathleen was so petite that people always thought her years younger. She was fascinated with the Alabama River and the boats and barges that plied up and down its waterways, often carrying goods to Mobile to be shipped around the world. She especially enjoyed seeing the steamboats. Occasionally they held passengers, and Kathleen loved waving at those on board who, in turn, would give a friendly wave to the sprite standing on the riverbanks.

Selma changed so much after the horrific war that ripped the nation apart. Cotton was no longer king, and Reconstruction made life in Dallas County increasingly difficult for a number of years following the war. Kathleen's innocent young mind could not conceive of her beloved country at war with itself, and people treating other people cruelly. Selma, long noted for its many beautiful homes and gracious style of living, slowly recovered from the damage inflicted by five years of war. Kathleen loved the elegant homes that lined the streets near downtown and Father's law office. She would walk down the street to his office, daydreaming about what stories those houses might be able to tell. A few structures had been burned during the Battle of Selma, but many were still intact.

Kathleen thought school was wonderful, not something to be endured but rather a treat to be enjoyed. Her nimble mind readily absorbed knowledge, and she quickly revealed a talent for memorizing. Reading was endlessly fascinating, and she quickly learned how to lose herself in the pages of a book. The young girl developed a tendency, even as a small child, for beginning her sentences with an adverb. Discerning friends and family members had noticed the same inversion of sentences when Louisa Mallory talked. It was a subtle way of taking the emphasis off of "I" and putting it on the other person. Kathleen's mother faithfully taught her youngsters the importance of putting others before themselves and listening attentively to the ideas of others. It became a lifetime habit for Kathleen, not just in the way she constructed her sentences but in the way she related to people as well.

September 1885 was a sad month at the Mallory house. Louisa

was expecting yet another child and went to Summerfield, as was her custom, so Clement Moore could deliver the baby. A baby daughter was born on the twentieth, but she did not live through the day. Kathleen, a perceptive six-year-old, read the sorrow on her mother's face, and it was a sight that burned deep into her heart. Thankfully, October of the following year was a time of sunshine and smiles, for tiny Irma Byrd Mallory joined the family. Irma was another dainty little girl, one who loved trying to do everything her big sisters did. The Mallorys now had a quartet of girls. Irma wanted to dance like Louise, or play games like Bessie and wear frills and lace like Kathleen. She especially loved playing "dress up" with Kathleen. Blues and pinks were Kathleen's favorite colors, and Irma thought her big sister was the height of fashion and wanted to be just like her.

Kathleen absorbed clothing *and* life lessons as she observed her parents and their deep love and respect for each other. One Easter morning when Kathleen was about eight, she overheard an interesting conversation between her mother and father as she was getting ready for church. Father had wanted to put on his second-best broadcloth suit, but he could not find it anywhere. Puzzled, he calmly put on an older suit instead and went downstairs. Finding himself ready early, Hugh decided to go for a short stroll in the garden to enjoy the warm spring day and collect his thoughts before teaching the Easter lesson to his large Sunday School class. Mother had gone into the garden to cut a few flowers for their table, and Kathleen, seeing them outside, decided to step into the garden for a few minutes herself. About that time, Colonel Mallory glanced across the fence in the direction of a whistling handyman from the neighborhood who was sauntering down the sidewalk about half a block away. Hugh stopped dead still and called to his wife, "Luta! Look there! That's Jim, walking down the street, and I could swear that is my black suit he has on!"

Louisa calmly kept cutting flowers as she responded, "Yes, Hugh. You see, he badly needed something to wear to church." Kathleen noticed that her father drew a deep breath, seemed to slowly let it out, and then commented, "Well, you might at the very least have asked your husband's opinion before you gave his clothes away!" With a little smile, she answered, "Yes, dear, that is true." And with a quick and blatantly obvious change of subject, she added, "Look at your roses here. I think they all probably need pruning. What do you think?" Kathleen noted that her father simply gave a little smile and obligingly acquiesced to the change in subject. It was a moment that stuck in Kathleen's mind and remained in her heart as an illustration of her parents' deep and lasting devotion to each other. She determined that one day she, too, would have such a loving relationship.

Lasting lessons from life in the Mallory home remained forever in Kathleen's heart. Especially precious were the Christmas memories. Mother always saw to it that everyone was excited about the most important event of the year, the celebration of the birth of Christ. She made sure every child had a special role to play in the family's celebration. Kathleen loved choosing and making gifts, wrapping them inexpertly but lovingly, and then finding a hiding place for the little surprises until Christmas. All the children loved helping decorate with evergreens and tasting plum pudding, Christmas cake and an assortment of fudge and candy.

She never really liked fruitcake, but she tried to be polite about it in front of the one who had cooked it. The children wrapped the banisters with garlands of holly and cedar and made wreaths for the large front door and the parlor mantel. The highlight of the season was never the opening of the gifts, fun though that was — but, instead, it was Christmas Eve. All would gather in the parlor around the glowing fireplace, its red embers crackling, and breathe in the fragrance of spiced tea wafting in from the large kitchen. There remained forever in her mind the glow, the fragrance and the sense of peace and joy as Father read from the Bible the Apostle Luke's account of the birth of the Christ child.

February 1889 ushered in another gift for the household, the birth of little James McInnis. In no time, he ruled the house. Big sister Kathleen had just had her tenth birthday, and this was like a living, breathing baby doll. Grandfather Moore commented that this time he delivered a "little man" to go with the four "little women" of the Mallorys. Until now, Hugh Jr. had been the lone male in the family. By the time James was two, he was talking in sentences and would happily command help from any family member, especially requesting that they fill his little apron pockets with delicious beaten biscuits.

Dallas Academy was close enough for the children to walk to school. Kathleen loved her classes and could never understand why some of her classmates complained about school and "all that drudgery." She found learning endlessly fascinating, and Louisa often had a hard time getting Kathleen to close a book at night and go on to bed. There was so much to read and so many adventures to explore in those pages. However, one particular subject was consuming a good bit of her thoughts. Always a deep thinker, Kathleen began to increasingly ponder on what she knew from family Bible reading and prayer time; from her Sunday School class with Mrs. Lamar, whom she adored; and from the messages she heard Dr. Frost preach each Sunday.

Considering with great seriousness her relationship with God, Kathleen spent long periods of time reflecting on what she knew about the purpose that brought Christ to earth and what that meant in her own heart. When dealing with deep and serious subjects, Kathleen tended to be introspective, and she already understood that this was one of those truly important things she must decide on her own. Louisa Mallory noticed that her Kathleen was spending a good bit of time on her own, and would often enter a room just to find her daughter sitting quietly — looking into the distance, as if in deep thought. Ever observant, Louisa realized the depth of the intellect of this child, and she decided to wait for Kathleen to come to her with whatever was on her mind. She would do that in her own good time, her mother was sure. But still, she wondered.

Louisa Mallory: Kathleen's mother

CHAPTER THREE

1889-1898

$\mathcal{B}$oth consciously and unconsciously, the Mallory children learned from their mother and father the meaning of duty. The biblical truth, "To whom much is given, of him shall much be required," was lived before the children each day. It was understood in the Mallory household that each child had certain responsibilities. Each was to carry his or her own weight and not take privileges for granted. As Kathleen matured, her mother noted in her an ever-growing depth of self-discipline. Louisa had never seen such earnest diligence in a child of Kathleen's tender years. She often mused that in years to come this might indeed be a driving force in the self-determination of this daughter. Time proved Louisa's uncanny wisdom.

Kathleen loved to help her mother when company came for dinner. She and older sister Louise were expected to assist their mother in setting the table, arranging a centerpiece of flowers from the garden, and serving dishes hot from the kitchen. Louisa handled responsibilities in such a way that the two older girls felt like it was an honor they had earned. The reward was being able to hear all the conversation from the interesting assortment of guests who frequented the Mallory home. Kathleen, in particular, loved to listen intently to all kinds of unusual and intriguing stories from visiting ministers. Prominent pastors often came to their Selma church for special services and then enjoyed gracious hospitality in the home of the prominent Mallory family. Other guests who were colleagues of her father — both those in law practices or sitting on the court, or, even more often, men who worked with Mallory on Baptist convention business. Hugh Mallory not only led a large Sunday School class in his home church but was also involved in Baptist work across the state.

Other times the Mallorys' guests were from their own church. Frequent among those were the women who worked with Louisa in the missionary society. Most of these were afternoon gatherings, where over cups of tea and some of Mother's lovely tea cakes, the women would discuss special needs in Selma and consider what they might do to meet those needs. Kathleen would listen and learn as she happily shared in serving tea to each lady and encouraging them to "have another of Mother's tea cakes." The youngster actually gleaned ideas that she could, in turn, share with her girls' missionary group as they made their own plans on how to extend helping hands. Kathleen and her friends — who were the older Sunbeams, sometimes called "Helping Hands" — enjoyed the privilege of having a leader who met exclusively with them as the "girls' missionary group." Kathleen adored Mrs. Betty and wanted to "be like her" someday.

First Baptist Church, Selma, was a pivotal part of the Mallory family. The children understood that unless they were really sick, they were to go to Sunday School, morning worship, evening worship, and prayer meeting on Wednesday evenings. Wednesday was the only time the Mallory children could spend less time on homework, and have a shorter piano practice time because there was prayer meeting to attend. Going to church was a way of life, not only for the Mallorys but for most of her friends as well. Church was something to look forward to each Sunday, for Kathleen idolized her teacher, Mrs. Lamar. Selma had four large churches very near each other — Baptist, Methodist, Presbyterian and Episcopal. Each had its own distinct steeple or tower, and most were constructed of red brick. Kathleen especially admired the arched windows, which seemed to point toward the heavens, as did the steeple on each sanctuary.

Dr. Frost, their pastor, was a frequent visitor at the house on Lapsley Street. James Frost depended heavily on the wisdom and depth of devotion of Mallory, one of his staunchest deacons and one he also considered a close personal friend. A Kentuckian, Frost was already a prominent Baptist minister prior to his call to the historic church in Selma. Young Kathleen formed many of her impressions about what an ideal pastor would be by observing and listening to her Selma minister. His brilliant messages were always theologically sound, but Frost was also intuitive enough to know how to make them understandable to lay persons, including children. Kathleen sat and absorbed those deep lessons each Sunday and loved the way her pastor used stories to illustrate biblical truths.

When Kathleen was but ten years old, Louisa discovered what was behind the periods of long thought that seemed to have become the norm with her young daughter. As was their custom, on this particularly bright new spring morning the family was gathered around the breakfast table. The four girls and Hugh were each in their usual seats, with little James asleep in his cradle. Colonel Mallory finished reading a chapter from the Bible and noted a specific passage in Matthew. "Children," he concluded their devotional time, "this is the verse I wish you to keep, 'Seek ye first the kingdom of God.' Don't ever forget that precept of the Master. Now," he concluded, "let us thank Him for His love and ask His guidance this day."

As soon as the prayer was finished, Kathleen quietly announced, "Father, I am going to join the church at the next service." Her voice was calm but very matter-of-fact. Hugh and Louisa exchanged a quick glance, and Hugh cleared his throat, "My child, this is a most important decision that must not be made in haste." Kathleen's bright young face and blue eyes became very sober. Brushing aside a vagrant curl, she turned immediately to her mother, her eyes asking the question. Louisa gently spoke up, "Kathleen, let's talk it over when you come in from school." Big brother Hugh had just been received for baptism a few months earlier, but, at fifteen, his parents considered him old enough to make such an important decision. Kathleen's parents wondered if her brother's profession had influenced this daughter, so young and so petite that she looked years younger. Could she clearly understand the significance of what following Christ truly meant?

Kathleen and her mother had a long, quiet talk that afternoon, with Luta amazed at the perspicacity of this young child. Together Kathleen's parents decided to make an appointment with their dear pastor and have Kathleen talk with him. The scholarly James Frost listened intently as Kathleen responded to his pointed questions, and within minutes he recognized the depth of her understanding and sincerity. Smiling gently at the precocious Mallory child, he suggested, "Talk to your parents, and plan to make your profession of faith next Sunday."

An excited young girl was ready before any of the family on Sunday morning. She carefully dressed in her favorite blue dress and put on her little flat-topped hat with ribbons at the back. Going into the garden, she discovered signs of spring all around her, from the jonquils by the fence to the deep purple violets lining the path. Kathleen stopped to inhale their fragrance and quickly decided that on this, the best of days, she would carry flowers to church. Picking a little bunch of violets, she was ready for the day. With Mother's help, she pinned the violets on her shoulder. As the invitation was given that morning, Kathleen walked calmly down the aisle to give Dr. Frost her hand. It was a day never to be forgotten. That night she was baptized. Being so small, Dr. Frost had to carry her in his arms into the baptismal pool. From that day on, there was a new sense of purpose about Kathleen Mallory, one that lay under all that she did. Her new commitment would have much to do with the future direction of her life.

Church, school and family consumed the time and interests of Kathleen and her siblings. Kathleen's decision to follow Christ ushered in a period of new seriousness of purpose, not changing her personality but deepening her perceptions and influencing the decisions she made. Family was the hub around which life revolved. Mother delighted their ears with stories of her childhood in Summerfield and compared life in those early days with life now after the cataclysmic war. Father talked of the early days when he finished law school and came to Selma to set up his practice. He grinned when he told his own mother's version of that journey. "Mama," he informed his eagerly listening children, "always told people I walked all the way to Selma, with only five dollars in my pocket. That's over a hundred miles. Actually," he informed them with a twinkle, "I came by rail, on the Rome to Selma line. But," he grinned broadly, "it's true I had very little money in my pocket! That was over twenty years ago, and that was when I met your mother."

When Kathleen was twelve, big brother Hugh went off to the Naval Academy. She missed him dreadfully, but thought him ever so elegant when he had leave and came home wearing his uniform. On more than one occasion, she thought that sometimes life didn't seem very fair. Why could not *girls* also have such exciting opportunities and venture out and see some of the rest of the world? She admitted to a bit of wanderlust in her blood, a thought she did not share with many. Eventually, Hugh decided the Navy was not the career for him and chose to return to the state and attend the

University of Alabama, as had their father. From all the conversations she heard, Kathleen decided that her brother would likely follow in their father's footsteps and become a lawyer as well.

Special joy entered the Mallory home while Kathleen was a teenager, but all too quickly turned to sorrow. In the summer of 1893, Louisa, already in her forties, rejoiced over the birth of their third son, naming him for her dear father, Clement. The tiny babe was alert and active, but so small and frail that any touch of a cold or illness greatly affected him. The little fellow fought valiantly, but a seemingly innocuous fever the next June was too much for his fragile constitution. The entire family grieved. Even years later, Kathleen's tender heart suffered a pang at the thought of her little brother Clement, gone too soon. It was an especially difficult year for the young seventeen-year-old, for just the month prior to her brother's death, the children lost their beloved grandfather, the one for whom the baby was named. Dr. Moore was eighty years old and had spent a lifetime helping the sick and bringing sunshine into the lives of his grandchildren.

Kathleen often buried herself in schoolwork, sometimes reading long after she should have been in bed asleep. Every subject was a delight at Dallas Academy, but her favorite was the classics. Textbooks were tough, and all the classes challenging. Kathleen excelled in Latin and relished mythology and ancient history. During her years at the academy, Colonel Mallory was involved in all sorts of civic endeavors in Selma, including being on the board of education. At the end of every school year, there was an awards day — and each time, Kathleen won the Latin medal, including her senior year. Hugh Mallory was beaming as he pinned the medal on her collar.

For all her seriousness in application to her studies, Kathleen was no "bluestocking." She was too fun-loving for that, and she loved fashion. Sometimes Louisa Mallory would smile as she saw Kathleen glance in a nearby mirror and brush her curls, or tweak her collar to look just so. She was also a most determined young woman, sometimes to the point of stubbornness. Kathleen could capably hold her own in a debate. Always listening to the opinions of others with courtesy and ever respectful of her elders, Kathleen nonetheless did not lightly change her mind, and her opinions, once formed, did not tend to vacillate.

This was especially true when coming to decide where to go to college. In the Mallory family, girls were just as challenged academically as the boys. Each was encouraged to go to college, and Kathleen was excited at the prospect. Several of her friends were planning to go to nearby Judson, one of the first colleges for women in the country. Judson was a wonderful school, but Kathleen simply did not want to go to college that near home. In later years, when there were countless times she wished she *could* be at home in Selma but was not able to, she thought back to that young Kathleen who couldn't wait to get out on her own. Although two large and prestigious state universities were located in Alabama, those as well were too close to home.

Kathleen's eyes cast further afield, and with her fine academic record, she could have her choice of institutions. Several alumnae of the Woman's College of Baltimore lived in Selma, and gave glowing reports of their alma mater that deeply impressed young Miss Mallory. She was so looking forward to the college world and being on her own. Hugh and Louisa were a bit taken aback when she made her college choice, but to their credit, they gave Kathleen the freedom to make her own decision. Older brother Hugh was her champion as well, thinking this would be a good thing for his sister. Both parents were loath to see their dear Kathleen so far away but warmed to the happy glow in her eyes as she looked forward to this next chapter in her life. They were prey to mixed emotions as they stood at the Selma depot that fall and waved an exuberant Kathleen off to Maryland and new horizons as yet unimagined.

Selma home where Kathleen grew up

CHAPTER FOUR

1898-1900

Stepping off the train in Baltimore, Kathleen stepped into a whole new world, one beyond anything she had encountered in her young life. Looking around with shining eyes, she was a welter of mixed emotions — a touch of trepidation because she was now on her own for the first time ever, and, equally strong, a sense of exhilaration, reaching out to grasp a new world of adventure and excitement. Being Kathleen, she had done her homework well and had learned a bit about what to expect in the big city. For a teenager from little Selma, Alabama, with its fewer than 10,000 people, to a thriving metropolis of more than half a million, was a vast contrast. Even the noise level was different, with the humming activity of hundreds of people busily going about their daily affairs. Kathleen had carefully read some of Baltimore's history and realized that she was certainly no longer in the Deep South. Baltimore had been a city of divided loyalties during the recent Civil War, with strong sentiment on both sides.

Boarding a streetcar for the first time was a novel experience, and Kathleen could scarcely keep her face sober and composed, as befitted a mature young woman traveling on her own. Despite her efforts, those sparkling blue eyes looked wonderingly at all the new sights and sounds of a thriving metropolis. The campus of the Woman's College of Baltimore (soon to be named Goucher College) was less than a mile from the train station, so Kathleen arrived at her destination within minutes of taking her first streetcar ride. She was now part of a student body of some 350 young women from Maryland and many other states. Actually being in college was a heady feeling for the ebullient Miss Mallory. The campus looked large to her, some eighteen acres in the middle of Baltimore. She had been assigned to a dormitory named Vingolf. Trained in the classics, Kathleen knew the meaning of the word that was borrowed from Norwegian mythology. She grinned to think of the name it gave all of its occupants: "the abode of goddesses."

Seventy girls lived in Vingolf, and Kathleen soon became a popular fixture in the dorm. The blonde curls of her childhood were now a shining light brown halo that topped a face with clear smooth skin and beautiful arresting blue eyes. Both petite and vivacious, she was nonetheless gracious and genuinely interested in her fellow dorm mates. Her fellow students noticed as well a refreshing air of humility about the winsome Miss Mallory, a lack of vanity that was both natural and unassuming.

Kathleen recognized the blessing that was hers in having come from a privileged family, and she determined not to take those blessings for granted. At the same time, it was lovely to have a bountiful wardrobe, and she filled her closet with suits, a number of skirts and puff-sleeved blouses, high-buttoned shoes, and plenty of petticoats with flounces. Mother had given her an evening dress with a frilly lace bertha, and her sister Louise gifted her with baggy bloomers for calisthenics.

Coming from a small town and graduating at the top of a class of nine seemed small preparation for a change of this magnitude, but Kathleen's foundation of high goals and of integrity went deep; consequently, her parents had been able to see her off with a sense of confidence, knowing the depth of character of this daughter of theirs. She quickly made friends in the dorm as well in her classes, and that first month she was elected president of the freshman class. Kathleen bought a shiny brass knocker for her door, and the room was open to one and all.

Although Goucher was a small school, it had several sororities, each of which rushed Kathleen. May Keller, a Baltimore native who became a lifelong friend, was assigned the responsibility of persuading Kathleen that she needed to be a Pi Beta Phi. All sorts of friendships developed with sorority sisters, but Kathleen had just as many friends outside her own sorority.

Goucher was steeped in the classics, which was a great fit for Kathleen, who favored studying the classics over any other discipline.

Latin was her chosen major, and her coursework included Horace, Livy, Pliny, rhetoric, and composition. Happy to take a full schedule, Kathleen also had a major in history, and a post-major in the Roman satirists. To balance out the classics, however, she included classes in math, chemistry, physics, and elementary anatomy. Kathleen only had one course in Bible, but the entire focus of Goucher was Christian in purpose, having been founded by Methodists. Attendance at church on Sundays was expected of everyone. All students attended a daily worship period on campus as well.

Classes did not consume all of Kathleen's time. She thoroughly enjoyed the newness of her college days, finding delight in visiting the city's museums and aquarium, as well as participating in games at sorority gatherings. It wasn't just her sparkle and natural beauty, but also her charming Southern accent that captivated those about her. Dorm life could be fun. In spite of dorm rules, which the students mostly endeavored to follow, they still managed to have fun and occasionally a bit of mischief. Kathleen was given credit for composing part of "Mother Goose Rhymes for College Geese":

There was an old woman who lived in a hall,
She had so many girls she didn't know them all,
Late at night she would find them all raising Ned,
Then she'd scold them with sadness and send them to bed.

Nonetheless, along with fun and weekend recreation, the bedrock Kathleen never changed. She loved fun, studied with awesome discipline, and continued to develop spiritually.

Kathleen was active in YWCA, as well as in a well-known Baptist church. On Sundays she and May Keller attended Eutaw Place Baptist Church, enjoying the streetcar ride that took them close to its doors. Eutaw's pastor, Rev. Julius Millard, had just accepted the pastorate of this historic church. Going to services there both sustained and fed Kathleen spiritually. There at Eutaw Place, Kathleen met the redoubtable Annie Armstrong, one of the founding "mothers" of Woman's Missionary Union, and a vital part of the ministry of the church. Miss Armstrong's Sunday School class was legendary, with anywhere up to 200 children attending each Sunday, ranging all the way from four to fourteen. Kathleen recalled her own little group of high school girls in the Selma church and wondered what they would make of a single class of 200.

Kathleen particularly admired Dr. Goucher, the college president. Everyone on campus benefited from his guidance. His residence was on campus, and the pastor of the large Methodist church, adjacent to the campus, lived just behind the Gouchers' garden. The two men saw each other most days, and, invariably, the parson greeted the president, "Well, John, what have you been doing for the kingdom today?" This question John Goucher, in turn, passed on to his students: "Ladies, what have you been doing for the kingdom today?" It was a mark of how much Kathleen admired him that she proclaimed his ideals like those of her beloved father. High praise indeed.

Kathleen was never at a loss for something to do. In addition to attending a full schedule of classes, studying in her dorm room or spending long hours in the library, Kathleen filled the remainder of her time attending services at Eutaw Place or participating in one of the many campus activities that enriched her life. The Agora debating society, sorority activities and assisting with the editing of *Kalends*, the school annual, were all a delight to the gifted young woman, now no longer a teenager. One afternoon in the Goucher library, she thumbed through past issues of *Kalends*, and smiled over memories it evoked: the snow battle between two of the dorms; the memorial service for Queen Victoria in 1901; a play, *London Assurance,* in which she played a part; the college boat ride on Chesapeake Bay; and the observance of the Victor Hugo Centennial. College life was all she could have hoped it to be.

The long miles between college in Baltimore and home in Alabama meant that Kathleen was seldom able to go home. By her junior year at Goucher, she looked back in her mind and smiled nostalgically at the girl who had been so eager to study far from home. She now wished that "far" wasn't quite as far. Those 900 miles between home and Baltimore loomed large at holiday times. Faithfully writing newsy letters home, Kathleen relished mail call, for Mother wrote each week, and Father was also a regular correspondent. Sometimes late at night, she would reread a special letter and an errant tear or so would well up her eyes.

Kathleen loved having lazy summers at home and each year particularly anticipated the Christmas holidays, when there was enough time to travel back and forth and still enjoy family time in Selma. However, she frequently found herself in a real home on weekends and enjoying family privileges because her dear friend May Keller lived in Baltimore, and the hospitable Keller home was wide open to Kathleen. She often enjoyed a welcome break from the rigors of many hours of studying to spend the weekend with May and her family and experience an atmosphere that reminded her of home. Sometimes the girls had dates on weekends and would go with their young gentlemen to off-campus sorority parties or concerts. Occasionally these gatherings were dances. Kathleen herself did not dance, but her friend May noted that she never lacked attention from numerous young men who preferred to sit and chat with the lovely girl with the intriguing accent. Young men from numerous universities in Baltimore particularly enjoyed the privilege of escorting lovely young students from Goucher, and May and Kathleen never lacked for entertainment.

Kathleen's world widened in Baltimore with all sorts of new experiences and challenges coming her way. However, she realized with each new adventure or temptation coming across her path that her spiritual roots went deep, and those verities that had been instilled in her young heart held firm and sure. The school's motto (in Latin, of course) — *Omnia probate; bonumn tenete* — was part of Kathleen Mallory's life ideal. It reads in 1 Thessalonians 5:21: "Prove all things; hold fast that which is good."

Kathleen applied to her college experience the same resolute habits of discipline that had been instilled in her heart from her early school years. Her roommate would sometimes glance over at Kathleen, diligently working away at her desk, never failing to complete an assignment before closing a particular book. Her friend noted Kathleen's neat desk, with its pile of tasks yet unfinished on one side, and completed work neatly filed away. Hour after hour, the unfinished stack would diminish in size, until it was finally cleared away.

One night, curiosity got the best of Kathleen's roommate and she asked, "How do you *do* it? How do you stick to a task so long?" Kathleen leaned back in her chair and gave a tired smile, "Discipline is just something drilled into this head of mine, I guess. I feel it is my duty, and Father always stressed to me the importance of duty in whatever I did." Then she continued with a rueful look, "And Mother always added that if I was going to do something, I needed to do it *right!*"

Her friend was curious: "I guess I never thought of *duty* much myself. It wasn't something stressed at our house." Kathleen explained, "We had family devotions each morning, and my father loved the passage from Ecclesiastes 12: 'Fear God and keep His commandments; for this is the whole *duty* of man.' You see," she continued, "Father loved to tell us of his *own* father who died the year before I was born. Grandfather kept a journal all his life, and it was full of his favorite phrase: Fear God and walk humbly." Kathleen paused for a reflective moment, then concluded: "I guess I heard this so many times, it just became a part of me."

On one particular weekend, Kathleen and a group of friends were invited to a dinner party in a Baltimore suburb. Kathleen later began to wonder if her hostess was a secret matchmaker, for shortly after the girls arrived, her hostess managed to introduce her to a handsome young man with a resolute chin. Janney Lupton attracted her at once with his flashing brown eyes and dark wavy hair. A recent graduate of medical school, young Dr. Lupton was just beginning his internship at Johns Hopkins, the renowned hospital located just a couple of miles from Goucher's campus. The attraction was instant and mutual, with Janney captivated by the beautiful smile and lilting voice of Miss Mallory. A short time later, Kathleen's hostess drew her aside with a touch on the arm, and whispered with a smile, "I knew you would like him. He has so much zest for living — makes me think of you!"

Kathleen was enthralled by Janney Lupton's accounts of his recent adventurous tour of Europe, and she listened intently as he told of sailing from Chesapeake Harbor on a cattle boat and touring Europe on his bicycle. His special delight was getting off the beaten path and biking around England, Belgium, Holland, France, Germany, and Austria. Janney's "sun bronze" made it evident that he was not long back from the trip, and he happily answered Miss Mallory's eager questions about sights he had seen along the way and people he had met. The young physician had already been to many of the places that Kathleen had only dreamed of seeing, and her fascination with his travels was genuine. Very evident to their smiling hostess was the fact that Dr. Lupton was in turn fascinated with the young lady eagerly plying him with questions. She felt quite sure that this would not be the last time these two had long conversations. And she was exactly right.

Kathleen Mallory in high school

CHAPTER FIVE

1900-1907

Long after the clock struck midnight, Kathleen was still lying dreamily awake in her bed, reminiscing over every part of the evening's dinner party. Kathleen had had her fair share of beaus and interested young men for quite several years now. That was nothing new. Her own reaction to such attention had never felt like this before, however. Janney Lupton was different. She smiled to herself, thinking how Grandfather Moore would have loved visiting with this bright young doctor. Her thoughts harked back to their conversation that evening and how his eyes flashed and sparkled when he talked about unusual adventures on his European tour. His resolute chin, refined, chiseled features, and lithe young form had printed themselves on her mind.

A highly popular young woman on her campus, always ready with a genuine smile and a kind phrase, Kathleen, nonetheless, was not one to openly express her innermost thoughts and feelings. They felt too personal to share. These exciting new thoughts of young Dr. Lupton certainly seemed too special to treat casually. With her usual iron discipline, the young college student went about her studies with both focus and fierce concentration, but found herself occasionally daydreaming and staring into space, making air dreams in her mind. Within a week, she and Janney had met again and quickly found ways to schedule their weekend free times to be at the same functions on numerous occasions. Their friendship blossomed, and both seemed amazed at how closely their ideas coalesced.

The Lupton household and that of the Mallorys varied in many ways, but at the same time, they had much in common. Kathleen's family life revolved around their Baptist church. Janney's family was thoroughly Christian, with his father, Edward, a strong Presbyterian and his mother, Mary Eva, a devout Quaker. Janney had two brothers; in fact, his younger brother McSherry attended the Friends School there in Baltimore. Not long after Kathleen and Janney met, he proudly introduced her to his beloved brother.

Of all Janney's interests, medicine topped the list. He was fascinated by his chosen profession and loved to talk of special cases he was studying at Johns Hopkins. Not only did Kathleen listen eagerly, she was also knowledgeable enough about medicine to ask pertinent and specific questions. Grandfather Moore had shared many a strange medical case with his fascinated young granddaughter.

Baltimore offered countless opportunities for amusement and mental challenge, from its museums to concerts and theatrical performances. A few months before Kathleen's graduation, the two attended a symphony concert on campus and slowly strolled in the direction of her dormitory following the evening's performance. And it was on this forever-remembered night that the two dear friends acknowledged that they were far more than friends. This was love. They were ready to commit to each other forever. Kathleen, her face aglow, softly suggested that because of his further medical preparation entailing both an internship and residency, that perhaps they would keep the engagement as their secret. She quickly added, "But not from our dear ones at home!" Janney saw the value of her idea, but neither of the two relished the thought of a long engagement. Nonetheless, the two sweethearts, quite convinced that no one had ever felt quite the depth of love that they did, decided that truly "love conquers all" and the ensuing wait would surely rush by. Kathleen carefully kept her word and told none of her sorority sisters or other close friends, but several of them were quite suspicious. The new luminescence in her radiant blue eyes was something of a giveaway.

Kathleen sat down the next evening to pen a long letter home. She started with a clean sheet of paper, then sat daydreaming over just how to share her wonderful secret. Quite a wordsmith, Kathleen finally composed a letter fairly screaming of her ebullient emotions. That letter left the Mallorys in no doubt that their beloved daughter was now head over heels in love.

Hoping that time would scurry on by and she could soon "live happily ever after" with the love of her life, Kathleen graduated with honors with a degree in the classics, specializing in Latin. She couldn't wait to get home and share face to face with Mother all the wonderful things about her young doctor, and "Mother, wouldn't Grandfather be more than delighted?" she bubbled, as she painted a glowing picture of her dear young man. "Yes, my dear child," Louisa responded, "Father would be so happy for you. And just like you," her mother smiled, "I miss his dear face and kind voice every day."

Determined to stay busy and thus help the days and months pass more quickly, Kathleen stepped right back into her role in the family. The letters flew back and forth, with Kathleen only sharing certain parts of her letters from Janney with her sisters. Her older sister Louise had married in January, and this September, 1902, brother Hugh married as well. Bessie, Irma and James were still at home. Kathleen felt right at home back in the church of her childhood. Mother was deeply involved in the missionary society, and Father was more than busy, with not just his flourishing law practice, but also serving as president of the Alabama Baptist Convention. Kathleen became involved as a leader with the Sunbeam Band and happily told the eager children stories of little ones in strange and distant countries.

Janney spent the summer in Germany, much of his time studying advanced surgical techniques in medical facilities there and further enriching his own medical skills. He loved the clean countryside and reveled in the opportunity to learn more in his chosen field. He then came back to Johns Hopkins to finish his senior year and teach in the night school of George Washington University as well as spend long hours at lectures and studying. Back in Alabama, Kathleen taught in nearby Demopolis during the week but normally spent weekends in Selma, attending her church and staying involved in its activities. Her students were fourth and fifth graders, with energy enough to keep the young teacher busy. Townfolk in Demopolis thought it a bit strange that such a pretty young teacher was not interested in a beau. The more Kathleen taught, however, the more convinced she became that teaching was not her particular calling.

Just after receiving his medical degree, Janney came South for his first visit to Selma. Kathleen had a fresh sparkle about her the entire time, and Janney was warmly received into the Mallory home. Strolling about town and visiting in Kathleen's church gave him a special feel for how deeply the entire family was loved and respected in their small city. Many evenings, he and Kathleen sat together in the front parlor, with young teenager James trying to eavesdrop when he got a chance. Kathleen knew her brother well, and to his frustration, they spoke too softly for him to ever listen in. One of Kathleen's favorite parts of Janney's visit was their day spent in Summerfield with Grandmother Moore, who sat for hours talking medicine with Kathleen's young man.

Just a few weeks later, Kathleen went for her first visit to Shadyside. The West Virginia countryside was lavish with lush green beauty that summer, and she savored long evening visits with Janney's gentle mother Mary Eva, eagerly asking questions about Janney as a little boy. Like everyone else, Kathleen was soon calling her "MissEvy." She saw much of Edward Lupton in his son and felt a close relationship with his parents. Brother McSherry added a special memory to their weeks together when he got hold of a bicycle built for two that allowed the happy couple to explore the countryside together. Janney's brother Will was also impressed with the radiant young woman now engaged to his brother.

The apple trees at Shadyside were fragrant, and Kathleen inhaled their sweet aroma during their moonlight strolls. It was a moment out of time — the two lovers walking slowly, savoring each moment and making plans for the years just ahead, when internship and residency were completed and the young couple could begin their lives together. Kathleen went to sleep each night with a smile on her face, hoping to have dreams about their happy and fruitful life together.

Janney returned to his internship and Kathleen to her teaching. The next year, when Colonel Mallory was returning from the Democratic Convention in St. Louis, he detoured by West Virginia in order to visit with the Lupton family. His days there left him happy about the choice his discerning daughter had made.

The time of Janney's internship was nearly completed when Kathleen received a shocking letter from her fiancé. It was a letter she never imagined, and certainly one she never wanted. She opened the fateful letter to read that her beloved was ill, actually quite deathly ill. After reading the devastating news, Kathleen at first sat in stunned disbelief. When she could gather her composure sufficiently, she went to find Mother. One look at Kathleen's ashen face, and her mother's heart plummeted. "My child, what *is* it? Are you all right?" In spite of her effort to control them, Kathleen's blue eyes welled with tears. "Mother, how can it be?" and she fell into her mother's arms, weeping. This was so unlike her composed and generally unflappable young daughter that Louisa was shocked. Kathleen haltingly shared the contents of Janney's letter, and Louisa began weeping sympathetic tears with her child.

Janney wrote that he had been ill for some time, but he had not mentioned it. He did not want to alarm his dear girl, and he had believed it to be temporary. However, a diagnosis had just been confirmed. The doctor assured him this was in the early stages and that meant there was much hope; however, the diagnosis was tuberculosis.

The very word struck terror to the heart. People called TB "the white plague" and many thought it a death warrant. Kathleen could do nothing but pray, pleading for healing and strength, and asking God to give them each one the grace they so sorely needed. How could this be? How *could* it have happened? Surely not. Louisa and Hugh spent long hours praying with their daughter, helping her work through the shock of such news. In his next letter, Janney wrote about Sir William Osler, his favorite professor. Dr. Osler came to him and advised that he receive treatment in the sanatorium in Saranac Lake, New York. Dr. Osler had a philosophy of healing that revolved around courage and trust, living in a spirit of gratitude, and, literally, taking it just one day at a time. His confidence was contagious, and Janney eagerly followed his prescription.

Dr. Trudeau, the founder and owner of the sanatorium, was himself a survivor of TB, prescribing for patients a therapy of rest and fresh air. Saranac Lake was in the beautiful Adirondack Mountains. Janney spent his days resting there, reading medical journals and the Bible, and each day he wrote Kathleen and his mother. Kathleen had been touched from the beginning by his tender devotion and attention to his mother. It told her a lot about the caliber of the man. Janney's letters were filled with positive thoughts, and the biggest heartache he felt was the fact that they must delay their wedding. It might be a long time before he was perfectly well.

Kathleen, in turn, faithfully wrote her beloved every day, filling her letters with little bits of news about life in Selma and her classes and pupils. Her sister Louise, who had married James Privett, had a little girl and named her Kathleen. Her aunt was both touched and thrilled to have such a beautiful little namesake. Mother was teaching her how to sew, she wrote, something she had never spent much time on in past years, and she had made a lovely new hemstitched tablecloth to put away in her hope chest. She was now leading the young ladies' missionary society at the church, and she enjoyed telling him about her experiences with the young teenagers and how they made her feel quite ancient, being a schoolmarm.

Janney's letters became increasingly optimistic as he was now well enough to be outdoors. That winter, even in the frigid weather, he sat in a deck chair, wrapped in a heavy buffalo robe and inhaled the crisp fresh air. As he grew stronger, Kathleen and her father went to New York to spend some time with him. The visit encouraged Kathleen's heart and gave her fresh hope. He was looking like himself again. He was healing. In 1906, Janney was finally pronounced completely well. He and Kathleen were jubilant. Now they could take their plans off hold and begin afresh. The young doctor was now through with his training, internship and residency, and was finally ready to start his practice. Expenditures were heavy, but the young couple was confident he would soon be established in his practice. That Christmas of 1906, the happy young couple decided on the date for their summer wedding in Selma.

Janney was working morning, afternoon, and often long into the night. He loved his profession and was eager to get firmly established and be able to begin his life with Kathleen. February came, and late one cold, wet afternoon and already exhausted after a grueling day, Janney was visited by a messenger, pleading with him to go see a poor young expectant mother who lived in a mountain cabin several miles away. Sighing, the tender-hearted Janney packed his saddlebags and mounted his horse to head to the mountain. There was a drenching cold rain, and he was soaked by the time he reached the cabin. Hours later and absolutely exhausted, he left, leaving behind a safe mother and her child. The rain had stopped, but the night was freezing cold, with a constant and penetrating north wind. The next morning, he was ill. He assured his landlady it was "only a pesky cough from exposure," and spoke bracingly, "Why, twenty-four hours in bed and I'll be fine."

Not a single day had passed since his college days that Janney had not sent his mother a daily card or note. But this week, several days passed, and not one letter reached Shadyside. MissEvy was immediately uneasy. Something was amiss. This wasn't like Janney.

She acted quickly: "Father, I know our boy is ill. Please send him a telegram and ask for an immediate answer." A reply came the same evening: "Forgive me for not writing. I have pleurisy but do not worry. Much love." Early the next morning, Edward Lupton drove into town and put older brother Will on a train headed to Hendersonville and their doctor son. Stopping by the post office on the way back to the farm, Edward found a letter from Janney's good friend, a Mr. Valentine, the editor of Hendersonville's weekly newspaper. Valentine wrote: "Your boy is desperately ill."

Will quickly brought his feverish brother home to Shadyside. Meanwhile, in Selma, Kathleen was experiencing deep anxiety. What could have happened? In two weeks now, she had received just one short note, and Janney wrote of his "slight illness." This was not like her Janney. Something was dreadfully amiss.

Her worst fears were all too true. The next day a telegram came from Janney's parents: "Come at once. Janney is ill." A shaken Kathleen immediately packed a few essentials and boarded a train for West Virginia. And for the entire month of March 1907, Kathleen sat at his bedside. With each passing day, her worst nightmares were slowly but steadily becoming all too real.

Kathleen Mallory's fiancé: Janney Lupton

CHAPTER SIX

1907-1908

*E*ver afterwards, Kathleen would recall the sharp living pain of anguish that ripped at her heart each hour of that last March of Janney's life. As she sat quietly beside his bed, holding his hand and speaking softly when he felt like talking, both of them tried to dwell on the lovely memories they had shared, moments of laughter and joy, reflections on the beauty of the time they came to realize their deep love and devotion to each other, talk of the plans they had made. Those were the moments that tasted as bitter as gall on the tongue, thinking on "what might have been."

It hurt too much, and the two decided without the thought even being expressed, that they could not keep speaking of such heart-wrenching plans that were now never to be. Occasionally, Janney's mother insisted Kathleen take a walk and stretch her legs, but those moments did not last long, for soon she would be back in his neat, airy room.

Each day Janney's face grew more gaunt, and each morning Kathleen's heart sank a bit more. How could it go deeper? There was no end to the depths of despair. On Saturday evening, March 23, as the sun was slowly setting outside the window, Kathleen, holding Janney's hand, felt his weak grasp of her fingers growing imperceptibly weaker with each passing moment, and as she gazed with welling eyes at his dear face, she saw his features relax and become still. His breathing stopped, and the love of her life slipped into eternity.

The memory of that final month was stamped indelibly into the texture of Kathleen Mallory's life, and she knew that an essential part of herself was forever gone. She sent a telegram to her parents and remained with the Luptons for the memorial service before making her sorrowful way back to Alabama. That train ride home passed in a blur. What now? All she had hoped for, planned for, dreamed about was forever gone. How could she possibly bear the pain? Kathleen's emotions did not show on the outside. She was too private for that. Yet the arrows of agony went right to her heart with shocking force. That final month together had been full of sacred sweetness, yet, at the same time, shrouded in sorrow. There was no replacement for such a loss. She must somehow learn to live with the pain and keep on moving and doing. She wanted to do nothing but scream and cry out, *Why? Why? Why?*

Kathleen's true source of comfort was her relationship with God and the depth of her sustaining faith. Nothing else answered the needs of her heart. Mother and Father knew her well, knew that tendency of hers to internalize pain, and they respected the privacy of her sorrow, going on about life in the Mallory home as normally as they could. The Psalms brought solace to Kathleen's heart, and she read dozens of them each day. Even as she sorrowed, Kathleen was grateful that she had decided to resign her teaching position last year in preparation for her wedding. Thank God. She did not think she could see the happy faces of dozens of nine- and ten-year-olds day after day, and, with a smile on her face, teach them as they deserved. Her sorrow went deep, but with her usual sheer, iron self-discipline, she maintained her composure in public. Those who knew her well could read the pain in her eyes, but most acquaintances noted only that the vivacious Miss Kathleen Mallory seemed a bit muted.

Kathleen's grief was a private grief, made possibly even more wrenching because she could not bring herself to share it with anyone, even her cherished mother and father. Long hours into the nights those first months, sleep was hard to come by. Kathleen would pray over and over, pleading for peace and acceptance of the stark reality of her loss. She would weep until the wrenching sobs would literally exhaust her, until finally the oblivion of sleep would overcome the anguish. Sometimes she would torture herself with thoughts of that little boy who would look like his father Janney, or the little girl who would run each evening to Daddy's arms. Only pain lay in those thoughts, and she often exercised sheer self-discipline, refusing to dwell continually on sorrow.

It was literally the depth of her faith that sustained her through those long months. Truths she had first learned as a little girl, assurances of God's presence and His peace, now slowly began to take on reality for her as she sought that presence and pleaded for that peace. Kathleen's Bible became her daily source of comfort. Additionally, spending time reading great writers also brought her a measure of escape. She had always been intrigued by the short, evocative poetry of Emily Dickinson and in her inner sorrow spent time delving into Dickinson's thoughts on death. Looking at a stanza of "I Measure Every Grief I Meet," Kathleen sat with tears gently slipping down her cheeks:

> I measure every Grief I meet
> With narrow, probing, eyes —
> I wonder if it weighs like Mine —
> Or has an Easier Size.

Slowly, slowly, the fog began to dissipate, and Kathleen was able to once more engage with others and have a semblance of normality. Never one day, though, did she fail to take a moment to send a note or a card to Janney's mother. MissEvy no longer had that daily act of thoughtfulness from her dear son, but Kathleen was determined to continue that same custom, and somehow ease the pain of that mother's heart.

A combination of things helped heal Kathleen's bleeding heart. The comfort of the known and familiar at home on Lapsley Street was solace. Summer came in full bloom, and she found beauty in the flowers and the quiet pace of life. Spending several days with Grandmother Moore was balm to her soul, and in worship at church she found a renewed sense of peace. More than ever in her life, Kathleen prayed, seeking not just consolation, but strength and much-needed grace, as well as direction in her life. She wanted it to count for something. Its direction had assuredly changed, through no choice on her part, but surely God had a special task for her.

Friends and family all seemed to have suggestions, each with the purest of motives, wanting to give a lift to Kathleen's heart. One friend declared, "You need to go abroad. That would be an amazing experience." Another well-meaning soul suggested that she go back to teaching, declaring, "There is nothing that refreshes the mind more than contact with little children." A small smile crossed Kathleen's face and she responded, "Maybe for some, my dear. I have already tried that." Then, with a twinkle in those blue eyes, she added, "You know, I am just too *bossy* for the schoolroom." And that was the end of that.

Inevitably there were many who speculated that Miss Mallory, possessing both youth and beauty, would in time acquire a new suitor, most likely more than one. Others, who knew her better, sensed that the devotion she had felt for Janney Lupton would not ever again be equaled in her heart. All the family rallied around their daughter and sister. Louisa and Hugh, knowing her so well, knew best what to say and what not to say, how to best comfort her heart and lift her spirits. Having brothers and sisters was a genuine blessing for Kathleen. By this time, Kathleen was enjoying quite a collection of little nieces and nephews: Hugh

Jr.'s two children, Hugh and Martha; and Louise's three, George, Hugh and her little namesake Kathleen. When Kathleen first held the tiny baby named for her, her heart was a mix of emotions. How precious, this beautiful little one named in her honor, yet she thought simultaneously of a little girl that she and Janney would never have. Her sister Bessie also had married and had little Jacqueline, now a bright, young three-year-old. Kathleen loved to hear the young nieces and nephews attempting to say "Auntie." Little tongues tried rolling around the word in their mouths, and it somehow came out as "Artie" (Ar-tee'). The name stuck, and ever after Kathleen was their beloved Artie. Yet another welcome distraction that first torturous year was the wedding of her sister Irma, who married Edgar Stewart in November.

In later years, Kathleen could look back on 1908 as the period where she began emerging from the weight of grief, the time when the divine direction of her life slowly began to take shape. Her brother Hugh, a lawyer now and a business partner with their father, was her steady comfort. He had many of their father's qualities and was attuned to the grief that had threatened to consume her, though those who did not know her well could not discern that struggle in her heart. Hugh was Sunday School superintendent, and he steadily worked at discovering church responsibilities for his cherished sister. Colonel Mallory was moderator of Selma Baptist Association now, and he was quite aware of her hesitancy to accept a responsibility in the county. Nonetheless, the nominating committee asked Kathleen to become superintendent of the county Woman's Missionary Union. Very reluctantly, she agreed, although her lack of enthusiasm was almost palpable.

Colonel Mallory did his part by joining her in visiting several of the rural churches, many of which had no missionary organization. It was up to Kathleen to help them organize, and somewhat to her own surprise, she rose to the challenge. Just getting to these country churches was a challenge in itself. Consider traveling by horse and buggy, often over long-established ruts, and combine that with frequent rain that just slowed everything down. This wasn't the biggest obstacle, however. That came in the form of the numerous small congregations where the "brethren" were not only opposed to missions; they were particularly opposed to "having any female speak out in the meeting house. It was against Scripture." Kathleen would frequently go in the daytime, and at noon, in a grove, gather together some of the women (of course, babies and children, too). She would talk about organizing a missionary society and explain how it would bless and support the church.

Despite her efforts, Kathleen often felt frustrated, seeing mostly difficulties and counting few real accomplishments. She noted one exception: For the first time, women's work was actually given an entire page in the association's minutes. It proved a left-handed blessing, for Kathleen admitted that there was precious little to fill the page. She also confessed to herself that she had not lived up to what the Lord required of her. She hadn't even lived up to what her father had hoped for. And with those thoughts, she realized that a new sense was stirring in her heart. She could no longer be content with just sliding along, feeling sorry for herself and being entirely too self-centered. There was no blinding flash of light, but Kathleen realized that she was awakening to what she had subconsciously pondered in her heart for many months: God *must* have a divine purpose for her life. She was not happy with the meaningless direction of these past months; she must search for what God had in mind.

Kathleen began filling each day, adding to her church work various activities around Selma. She joined in the functions of her literary club and accepted numerous invitations to luncheons and teas. Kathleen enjoyed concerts with friends and her family, and even attended some stage productions. Yet, even as she participated, that divine discontent crept into her mind and heart. These pursuits were entertaining but strangely unsatisfying. Kathleen grew increasingly aware that she could not be content with merely passing the days in pleasure with an occasional attempt at doing good. She finally sought the answer from God, longing for Him to open her eyes to what He wanted for her.

That spring of 1908, Kathleen went with her father on a short trip to the country, not any great distance out of town. Spring was just beginning to assert itself, and as the two rode along in the buggy, they noticed the trees beginning to sprout buds and the little green shoots pushing up through the hard soil. Passing a barren patch of field, Kathleen voiced her question: "Father, why is that field bare, with nothing growing there?" Mallory responded, "There are times, Kathleen, when it is best to let a field lie fallow for a season. Then you can have seed sown and it will yield a better crop than ever." And there began growing in Kathleen's heart a new awareness of this fallow period of her life, and a sense that God might be using this inactive season to prepare the soil of her soul for what He would plant there.

Colonel Mallory had remained very active in the state Baptist convention following his five years as president, and this year he urged Kathleen to attend with him. She had never been to a state meeting and readily agreed to go, thinking it would be interesting to watch her father in his various roles with the convention. Hugh Mallory wisely suggested that his daughter help with the women's meeting that took place at the convention each year. Her role would be to read to the ladies a letter from their missionary in Shantung, North China, who worked with the legendary Lottie Moon. Anna Hartwell had written a vivid letter describing the hard life of women in China's interior, women who had never had the opportunity of hearing the good news. Upon first reading it, Kathleen was impressed with its vivid account of life half a world away, and, realizing that this would take little prior effort, readily agreed to read it at the meeting.

Then another request arrived for Miss Mallory. Would she serve as chair of the enrollment committee for the women's sessions? And, again she agreed, even as it crossed her mind that things were happening rapidly. The state convention that year of 1908 was held in Roanoke, Alabama, a quiet little town of some 3,000 souls. Since the town boasted only one small inn, all Baptist families living in town and the surrounding countryside were asked to open their homes to accommodate the 450 delegates. Baptist homes rallied around and helped house the guests, as did a number of kind Methodist friends in the community.

No chicken was safe around Roanoke for a couple of weeks in July. Countless fried pies, cakes and pies were prepared in busy ovens all over town. Hugh and his daughter were among a fortunate twenty delegates welcomed to the home of Deacon Carter Wright and his wife, Alma, the backbone of First Baptist Church Roanoke's missionary society. And that day was born a friendship ordained by heaven, for Alma Wright became the close and lifelong friend of Kathleen Mallory.

In fact, the entire week was a turning point in Kathleen's life, a moment in time when she began to literally sense God at work in her life's direction, and for the first time in more than a year of working through grief, there appeared before her a budding sense of purpose and a future with meaning.

Kathleen Mallory at Goucher College

CHAPTER SEVEN

1908-1909

*K*athleen would have been astounded had she known that this, her very first state convention, was the beginning of conventions and meetings that would fill her life for the next forty years. On this humid July evening in Roanoke, she was greatly impressed by their hostess, Alma Wright. Not much older than Kathleen, she was both gracious and charming, not appearing a bit flustered even with a houseful of guests to entertain and three young children bouncing around. Kathleen was especially taken with little Annie, a bright five-year-old who very importantly assisted her mother by running errands. Kathleen discovered that Alma was the backbone of their local missionary society and played a big part in preparations for the women's meeting of the convention. Ladies were scheduled to meet in the Methodist church the following day while the men of the convention met across the street at First Baptist.

That opening night, all delegates and visitors met together, but the next morning, Kathleen made her way with Alma Wright to the women's opening session. Picking a middle pew, Kathleen feasted her eyes on the lofty Gothic choir loft and the beamed ceiling before gazing at the four beautiful stained-glass windows, each depicting a different figure of Christ. Next, her soul was refreshed with the melody of women's voices raised in praise. Gazing around at all the women from churches small and large across the state, Kathleen experienced a new sense of awareness of the strength and vitality of her denomination.

Jessie Stakely, wife of Charles Stakely, pastor of the historic First Baptist Church of Montgomery, was presiding. Alabama's state WMU president, Mrs. Stakely had spent five years as national president, serving alongside Annie Armstrong in leading Baptist women across the country. Kathleen was deeply impressed with her gracious manner and fluid presiding skills, as she kept every-thing moving like a well-coordinated machine. When introducing state leadership, Jessie Stakely asked Kathleen, as chair of the state enrollment committee, to stand, introducing her by saying, "Miss Kathleen Mallory, daughter of our well-known Baptist layman, Colonel Mallory of Selma."

So typical of women everywhere, a little murmur of whispers could be heard with comments like, "Isn't she pretty in that pale gray silk and that hat with the rosebuds," and another: "I hear that she has worn a lot of gray since the death of her betrothed." Kathleen seemed oblivious to the murmurs around her and listened intently to a number of reports and messages. She didn't need convincing that the Great Commission was *her* commission as well, but she was energized by the realization of the far-reaching influence of Woman's Missionary Union and its continually expanding ability to reach the world for Christ.

However, on the second morning of the meeting, a remarkable thing happened in her heart. As Kathleen rose to read the letter from North China, speaking aloud the words of Anna Hartwell — words telling of the crying needs of Shantung Province and of the ministry she shared with Lottie Moon — it was as if her own eyes were opened and she could literally *see* those beseeching, needy souls. With this public reading, Kathleen's heart was directly touched. It was a moment out of time, as if a voice spoke in her ear and she knew she was ready for the rest of her life to begin.

Those women in Roanoke had no way of knowing the transformative moment that had come to Kathleen Mallory, but they were very aware that she had stirred them in some unusual way, and it was like an instant love. Following the morning session, her name was repeated over and over, with remarks like: "Was not she fairly aglow as she read that letter?" And another, "Oh, my, what a worthy daughter of that worthy father," and yet another, "I wish she could come and speak to the women and the girls in our church."

Two major changes came out of that Roanoke meeting. First,

the women voted to hold their annual meetings in November, at a different date from that of the state general convention. The second significant event was *not* recorded in the meeting minutes but in Kathleen's heart — what she later described as "the sudden unfolding of my mind and heart to world missions as I read Miss Hartwell's letter to the audience." Later that evening, Kathleen had an opportunity to spend some time with Alma Wright and express a bit of her feelings, and on that weekend the two formed a bond and friendship that lasted for the remainder of their lives.

Early in September, the state WMU executive board asked Kathleen to become volunteer leader of the Young Woman's Auxiliary of Alabama. And therein began an official involvement that never ended. Working from home in Selma, she wrote letters to all newly organized YWA groups and carried on regular correspondence with groups already at work. Additionally, she spent a great deal of time compiling reports and wrapping countless packages of material for mailing to the various YWA organizations. Her first open letter to all Alabama YWAs appeared in the *Alabama Baptist* on October 6, 1908. It was full of practical suggestions and assurances of her willingness to help each auxiliary, concluding, "We have a gloriously busy year mapped out for us, and of course we are going to fully measure up to it."

Since the annual meeting date had been changed, there was just a short three-month interval between the two gatherings. Kathleen's report for her first two months as volunteer director was nothing short of amazing: 1,125 miles traveled, three institutes attended, 154 cards and letters mailed, 369 packages of literature mailed, and articles for two pages in the *Alabama Baptist.*

Jessie Stakely presented a challenge to the women: "Let us advance on our knees." Kathleen made a personal vow that not only on her knees but with her hands and heart and soul she would seek to move forward and lead others to do the same. Having long been taught about prayer and seen it daily modeled in her home, Kathleen's own prayer life now took on new dimensions. A new missionary prayer calendar had been started by Miss Fannie Heck, the national president, and it contained the names of all their missionaries, both home and abroad, as well as convention leaders. Kathleen kept her copy close at hand and looked upon those names as a time of divine encounter in intercession for these who were committed to sharing the hope found in Christ. From that time on, every morning for more than forty years, Kathleen knelt to pour out her heart in intercession for God's messengers.

From knowing just a little about the wider world through her girls' missionary society in Selma and her involvement with small WMU groups in her association, Kathleen now recognized a whole new world of missions — and the vast network put into play by remarkable women of vision. She had met the legendary Annie Armstrong in her Baltimore church, of course, but had not realized the depths of that pioneer woman and her vital role in the very structure and foundation of the organization. After all, WMU was only twenty years old, and it was continuing to expand and develop. She was just now beginning to understand something of WMU's inner workings and of the thought, prayer and planning that went into it.

Kathleen's enthusiasm was contagious. Everything about Young Woman's Auxiliary was new and fresh, and the YWAs of

Alabama were entranced by their young and beautiful leader. She pored over every issue of *Foreign Mission Journal*, paying special attention to the practical suggestions appearing on the page written by Miss Fannie Heck. Kathleen was looking forward to her first opportunity to meet Miss Heck. She had learned from Jessie Stakely about the remarkable abilities of their leader. All who knew her called Miss Heck "the most beautiful Southern Baptist woman," and Kathleen, having seen a portrait of her, readily agreed. She was eagerly anticipating the time when she could personally become acquainted with Miss Heck. Although Heck had just returned to the office of president two years earlier, she had already begun a magazine, *Our Mission Fields*, for women and YWA girls.

Kathleen's new beginning seemed to be reflected in the very air and tenor of the nation. Progress seemed to be everywhere, and the South was leaving behind some of the inevitable sense of discouragement that followed the devastation of internecine war. Selma had used mule-drawn tramcars for years, and now these were replaced by electric trolleys. Even more progressive, automobiles were becoming more popular. City leaders, the local paper reported, were quite concerned with the unnecessary and reckless speed many thoughtless motorists risked in downtown Selma, some going over ten or even twenty miles an hour. Accidents were becoming far too common. Kathleen's friend Alma Wright wrote about the addition in their household: "What do you think? My husband bought us a White Steamer. It's the first car in Randolph County. The horses are usually frightened as we pass!" Alma ended her letter, "I hope to carry you in it to the youth rally next month."

Such meetings were becoming common for the busy Kathleen. She did nothing half-heartedly, spending many hours in preparation, travel and promotion of YWA work throughout the state. From the point where she felt the call of God on her life, she did not hesitate to attempt any service for Him. Kathleen was excitedly anticipating the next state meeting being held in Selma; for once, she wouldn't need to travel. Shortly before the November meeting, the state WMU nominating committee contacted Kathleen, asking if she would allow her name to be submitted as WMU corresponding secretary for the state of Alabama. Kathleen was shocked when she first opened the letter and read its contents. Shock was quickly replaced by a sense of inevitability. Had she not committed herself unreservedly to do whatever task it was that God might have for her? She agreed that her name could be offered in nomination for the position, wondering with a little thrill of anticipation just what might lie ahead.

Both Hugh and Louisa Mallory sat in the sanctuary of their home church that night of the meeting, and their hearts swelled with joy as they heard the name of Kathleen Mallory presented as the committee's recommendation to serve as the state's WMU director. Kathleen had just had her thirtieth birthday, but the ladies of Alabama glimpsed in that glowing young woman a depth of maturity and a winsome spirit that defied the calendar. The presence of several special guests also made the meeting evermore memorable for Kathleen. Alabama's Willie Kelly, long-time missionary to China, was home on furlough; she spoke at the annual meeting and enjoyed a delightful evening in the gracious

Mallory home, along with Edith Crane, national WMU secretary. Crane had succeeded Annie Armstrong and was providing quiet and thoughtful leadership. Edith was also particularly observant, and what she saw and heard of young Miss Mallory made a deep impression on her.

As soon as the final session closed, Miss Kelly, Edith Crane, and Kathleen traveled the short distance to Judson College in Marion. Judson was the place where the first-ever Young Woman's Missionary organization had been formed the year the college was founded in 1838. Most appropriately, it was named the Ann Hasseltine Judson Young Woman's Missionary Society, just as the college had been named for America's first woman missionary. Miss Kelly had worked many years before in the Alabama Mission Board office right there in Marion and had been an active member of the society, so this was like old home week for her. Kathleen was fascinated with the message Miss Kelly brought, telling of the blessings of sharing the gospel for the past fifteen years in Shanghai. Right there, a special bond was formed — and Miss Kelly became Kathleen's "special missionary friend," and the two remained in close touch the rest of their lives.

A brand-new challenge lay before the new state secretary. Alabama's WMU established its headquarters in Montgomery, and Kathleen was thrilled to be able to count on the wisdom and expertise of Jessie Stakely as she began her new task. Stakely's vast experience and brilliant mind were wonderful assets, and both Charles and Jessie Stakely were deeply impressed with not only the enthusiasm and charm the young Miss Mallory brought to the office, but her deep intelligence, breadth of knowledge and awesome self-discipline astounded them as well.

Alabama women happily furnished their new mission rooms from which material and plans would go out across the state. Their new secretary found her new office comfortable, but she saw right away that she was not going to be working in a restful atmosphere. There was far too much to do for that. She quickly realized the magnitude of this new responsibility. Here was a fresh challenge, and Kathleen Mallory loved challenges.

Kathleen Mallory in 1912: Age Thirty-Three

CHAPTER EIGHT

1909-1912

athleen felt a wonderful sense of new beginnings — new office, new challenges, new goals. She was well aware of God's special favor in the remarkable mentor He had provided: Jessie Stakely. Here Kathleen was, completely untried in a new position, having to learn from the grassroots up, but being blessed to learn from the woman who had led Baptist women nationally for years. Jessie Stakely's great good sense, her wisdom and her years of experience brought Kathleen up to speed in a hurry. And it was providential that she could now attend the great First Baptist Church of Montgomery and feed on the messages of Charles Stakely.

For her part, Jessie Stakely was astounded at the keen mind and business acumen of the petite and deceptively quiet Miss Mallory. She could turn out an incredible amount of work in a short time, methodically working through each stack of work she had piled high on her desk. Within a few short months, WMU women across Alabama, plus scores of pastors, were referring to Kathleen Mallory as "that fine little businesswoman." The task before her became increasingly clear as she noted that of the 1,963 Baptist churches, both small and large, less than 450 even had a WMU, and fewer still had the children's organizations. Letters, visits and the sharing of ideas and inspiration all began flowing from the vitality of the new state secretary.

However, Kathleen never talked publicly about the loss of her beloved Janney. There were many who did not know her well who were prone to think that she was "completely over him." They could not have any idea how his loss went deeply into the very fiber of her spirit. Nor could they have known that for the next ten years after his death, each night in the quietness of her room, Kathleen wrote a note to MissEvy, Janney's mother. Until Mrs. Lupton's death in 1917, not once did that lady find an empty postal box. The two women shared a sacred bond. Just as Kathleen never began a sentence with "I," she never openly revealed her grief; instead, she kept it quietly buried deep in her heart.

Kathleen's fashion sense was another reflection of her quiet decorum. Nearly everything she wore to the office was some shade of bluish gray. The color beautifully enhanced her long-lashed eyes of blue. The fashion of the day dictated using detachable white pique collars and cuffs, and, in the early years, those collars would be stiffened with whalebone. For travel, Kathleen packed her blue-gray outfits, shiny black-buttoned shoes and black gloves. For church, Miss Mallory's gloves of choice were white, and never was she seen without a pair, or without a lovely lace handkerchief. Nothing about her appearance was flashy or conspicuous, but with her curling hair and a bright face that so often wore a smile, no one accused her of being dowdy or frumpy.

Kathleen quickly grasped the magnitude of the task of WMU and the joy of feeling a sisterhood with women across the "Union," as Southwide WMU was so frequently titled. She gained expertise in her role by attending WMU's annual meetings and learning from directors in other states who had years of experience in leading women. Especially, she was amazed at the skill and power of the presentations of Miss Fannie Heck. The Union president was loved by all, and her powerful annual messages were the highlight of each year's gathering. Kathleen's first national meeting was in Baltimore, and it was a double thrill: not just being a part of the corporate body of WMU, but being able to return to the city of her wonderful college years — the place where she had met the love of her life. Miss Heck took note of the lovely young Miss Mallory and observed the way she interacted with others — absorbing, listening and quietly adding her own well-thought-out ideas. The 1911 meeting the following May was in Jacksonville, Florida. There, Miss Heck and Edith Crane introduced the concept of a Standard of Excellence by which WMU organizations could plan and implement their work. Kathleen's keen and methodical mind quickly picked up on the idea. It sounded like this would be a way she could challenge the women in Alabama to organize and enlist other women and youth in missions involvement.

As she traveled to countless churches and to association meetings across Alabama, nothing was more encouraging to Kathleen than to note the way women developed their leadership abilities. She happily told her mother of the thrill it was to hear a woman who just a year earlier would not dare speak in public but who now could pray in public and give her testimony, or stand on her feet to lead a group. Young Kathleen felt a bit like a mother hen when older women in the Alabama "flock" began to recognize their own potential. Every woman had a special knack, and Kathleen resolved to help each of them find what their own particular strength might be.

News from home was an energizing force for Kathleen, especially during her second year at the new position, when Colonel Mallory decided to run for governor. He was highly respected, not just in Selma but literally around the state. Kathleen secretly thought that anyone would be foolish not to vote for her wonderful father. In her daydreams, she could picture Father in the governor's mansion in Montgomery, right in the city where she now lived. Nevertheless, the politics of the state and the issues of the time worked against Colonel Mallory. He was strongly opposed to liquor and supported prohibition. The leading newspaper, the *Montgomery Advertiser*, confessed, "Mr. Mallory is the man most eminently fitted for and deserving of the office, and frankly admits that it had intended to support him, but it cannot forgive him for the one error of differing with it on the prohibition amendment." Thus, based solely on his Christian stance, Hugh Mallory was defeated in the race for governor. He retired from politics altogether; henceforth, all of his investment of time and energies were given to his church and to the Baptists of Alabama. His daughter grew spiritually as she marked the grace and lack of bitterness with which her father dealt with defeat.

Meanwhile, Kathleen — being Kathleen — was winning friends across the state with her charm and genuine concern for others. She was learning on the job, and her skills were developing exponentially. The members of her Montgomery church adored the captivating young woman who had quickly stolen their hearts. Pastor Charles Stakely was credited with giving her a nickname which forever stuck: Kathleen Mallory, the Sweetheart of Alabama Baptists.

Growth in Alabama's WMU had been immediate. Kathleen was happily gratified when Alabama Baptist women realized that another staff member was necessary. In just her second year, Kathleen needed help in the office. Laura Lee Patrick, a recent graduate from the WMU Training School in Louisville, was chosen to be the young peoples' secretary. The two young women worked well together and decided to set up light housekeeping in a little apartment near the office.

It didn't take Laura Lee long to discover the incredible work ethic of her new boss. Late one night, the two were working on the annual report that was to be sent to Baltimore to Edith Crane. With a staff of two people, all the paperwork, correspondence and bookkeeping fell on them. A few minutes before midnight, Kathleen leaned back at her desk, stretched her neck and tiredly rolled her head around to give it a rest. Laura Lee glanced up at the clock, gave her roommate a look, and asked, "Will we *ever* get through? It will be midnight in five minutes!" Kathleen nodded in agreement but explained: "Laura Lee, I've got to recheck the gifts from two associations. Hand me that file, please."

"Did you credit the dollar that the lady in Mobile sent last week?"

"Yes, and I wrote her a little note on the receipt I included."

"But, Kathleen, there is no need to carry on personal correspondence with *everybody!*"

Kathleen came back, "But you never know *which* woman might, with a bit of encouragement, find a place of great usefulness."

The work continued on into the wee hours. At about 2:00 a.m., Laura Lee had to stop a few minutes and before she knew it, she had dozed at her desk. Shaking her head, she went back to work, but around four o'clock she literally fell asleep. Kathleen never would tell her what hour she finally finished. She smiled happily over their morning cup of chocolate, enjoying the feeling of a job accomplished. Meanwhile, Laura Lee marveled all over again at the core strength and spirit of the gracious young woman who led Alabama's WMU.

Another habit of Miss Mallory's that captured Laura Lee's attention was her prayer life and her mode of prayer. Sharing a tiny apartment was a way to really get to know someone. Prayer, to Kathleen, was as natural as breathing. At first, Laura Lee was surprised to see that as Kathleen prayed each morning and evening, she knelt to voice her petitions. Laura quickly realized how natural this was to her roommate, something that she must have been doing for years. When the two prayed together, Laura

Lee noted that her friend's prayers were as confiding and natural as the conversation of a child with her father.

Meanwhile, changes were coming to national WMU, headquartered in Baltimore. Edith Crane, who had replaced Annie Armstrong following her retirement, was still a young woman, but her constitution had never been strong. She had been leading WMU for less than five years, but her frail body could not sustain the travel and rigors the office demanded. Her doctor advised complete rest. Crane most reluctantly informed the executive committee that she must resign her position, effective January 1912.

Kathleen had just begun her third year as Alabama's corresponding secretary when the letter from Miss Heck came. To receive a personal letter from WMU's iconic president was an absolute surprise to the unpretentious Kathleen Mallory. There was a genuine spirit of humility that existed in her; it was both natural and unassuming. She had not been aware that Miss Heck would even remember having met her. Yet, in this letter, Fannie Heck was actually asking Kathleen Mallory to assume the helm of Woman's Missionary Union as its new corresponding secretary. The shock sent Kathleen sinking into the nearest chair.

Here was WMU's paragon of a president, with many years of experience, full of visionary ideas and amazing powers of persuasive speech, asking her — young Kathleen Mallory, a fledgling state leader — to come to Baltimore and work alongside Heck herself. WMU was one of the world's largest organizations for women, an institution with the potential for incredible growth and limitless service. And Miss Heck and the nominating committee actually felt that *she* could lead them?

It did not seem possible.

Kathleen immediately wrote to her parents. They, who knew her best, could surely help her think this through. Her mentor Jessie Stakely was delighted when Kathleen haltingly told her of the call to lead WMU. Knowing the Union and its inner workings as she certainly did, Stakely quickly assured Kathleen that she had full confidence in the committee's choice and in her young friend's strength and depth of character, her proficiency and organizational skills, and most of all her deep-seated faith.

Together with Laura Lee, each evening as they prayed together, Kathleen repeatedly asked God for wisdom and guidance. After a week where Hugh and Louisa prayed together about Kathleen's decision, her father wrote of their conviction that she had those qualities needed for such a challenge, telling her: "It is a call to you to a high and responsible position. If you accept it, the moving reason on your part must be that of duty. You will be taken away from us in large measure and from the state work, but if duty calls, it must be answered. It is your life work. I wish you to do that which is best, which our Master would have you do." There was no doubt in her parents' hearts that God was leading Kathleen to this position, one for which He had been preparing her for many years.

Kathleen delayed her answer to Miss Heck. Her heart had to be certain. This was a matter that would surely determine much of the future trajectory of her life. Kathleen decided to write her dear Dr. Frost. Although he had left the pastorate in Selma the same year he baptized her, he had remained a close friend of the Mallory family and was much interested in their lives. He was now executive secretary of the Sunday School Board, and Kathleen highly valued his opinion. He knew the depth of spiritual maturity in this young woman. Frost answered her letter: "You have so many qualifications and special fitnesses for the work as if the Lord had just been training you for it."

And yet again she prayed with Jessie Stakely, earnestly seeking God's direction. Then, as if that inner voice spoke assurance to her heart, she knew the answer she would give, and peace surrounded her. That day, Kathleen sent a telegram to Fannie Heck. She would accept the responsibility. Without delay, she must adjust her mind and heart to the changes that were bound to come. And now, more than ever in her life, she recognized her utter dependency on her Heavenly Father. This calling was beyond her own capabilities.

Kathleen Mallory at her desk in Baltimore.
Above the desk hangs a picture of her
beloved missionary friend, Willie Kelly.

CHAPTER NINE

1912

*E*ver after, that sacred morning in Oklahoma City was stamped on Kathleen's memory, and running through her mind, as if watching a scene unfold before her, she could recall the sequence of events of that pivotal year. Here she was again, standing on the threshold of a new beginning. These months working with women in Alabama had been fruitful and rewarding. Picking up stakes so recently put down and plunging into the unknown would not be easy. However, with her usual commanding discipline, Kathleen went about completing her office work in Montgomery and leaving material and plans in order for whoever would succeed her. Her roommate helped her prepare to leave for Oklahoma City, getting all the clothing and accessories ready so Kathleen could focus on the occasion itself. Dresses, gloves, hat, all were prepared in ample time. At the top of her small steamer trunk, Kathleen carefully laid the dress she would wear for her formal election. And nestled next to it was a treasured gift, the new Bible given her by Grandmother Moore specifically in honor of this auspicious occasion. Kathleen smiled to herself as she folded the dress. This time it wasn't the usual gray or soft blue. It was a delicate shade of yellow, a bit like a touch of sunshine.

Fannie Heck, with her usual attention to detail, had carefully planned the program. She asked Miss Mallory to lead the devotional messages at the 1912 meeting, thereby giving women who did not know her an opportunity to get a look at the lovely young woman from Alabama. Hundreds of women heard her speak, sharing deep spiritual truths in her rich voice and in a manner that showed those truths to be straight from her heart. Kathleen might appear delicate and dainty, but her words were powerful and her message pointed. Attending the annual meeting were a handful of women who had been at the historic organizational meeting of Woman's Missionary Union in Richmond in 1888. Now, twenty-four years later, they were here in Oklahoma City, part of a new era with a fresh, young, new leader.

Eliza Broadus was one of that handful. Daughter of the famed professor and seminary president John Broadus, Eliza was indubitably one of WMU's "founding mothers." She was also chair of the nominating committee and totally convinced that Kathleen Mallory was God's person for this strategic position. The highlight of the meeting was to be the election of a new corresponding secretary, and anticipation was building. Kathleen admitted to herself, even as she sat in a calm and meditative state, that the vast significance of this moment to the rest of her life was an overwhelming experience. It was a bit as if she were standing at some distance and viewing in a dream what was taking place. Shortly before her name was to be placed in nomination, a note was slipped to her hands. It was Eliza Broadus's card, and on it she had written, "I think you will like to know that you are the unanimous choice of our committee." Kathleen's heart skipped a beat and a tremulous smile crossed her face.

When Miss Heck invited her to the podium, Kathleen gracefully rose and moved in that direction. As she made her way to the platform, one worthy older WMU matron leaned over to whisper to her neighbor, "There's just one thing I don't like about her." Puzzled, her friend frowned and inquired in surprise, "What is *that*?" "She's too young," the matron answered on a smile.

Fannie Heck called on the chair of the nominating committee for their recommendation, and Eliza Broadus reported the selection of Miss Kathleen Mallory, noting that she "possessed high qualities of mind and heart." The congregated women overwhelmingly elected their new corresponding secretary and Kathleen calmly accepted, promising her devotion to the task to which she had been called. She concluded in her rich, slow voice, "Let us pray." To the surprise of many in the congregation,

Kathleen very quietly sank to her knees there on the platform, her yellow organdy skirt settling around her, and reverently invoked God's blessings on WMU and vowing to Him her total commitment to the task. And ever after, those women from across the nation remembered that sight of their Miss Mallory reverently kneeling to pray. The prayer that May afternoon was remarkable, for in words as simple and confiding as those of a child, Kathleen talked with her Heavenly Father, asking Him to give his blessings on the years ahead.

The women of WMU were captivated by their radiant new leader. Soon, each came to recognize her genuine humility. Clearly her strength was rooted in her prayer life, and it made an impact on the great effectiveness of her work from its very inception. Even on that beginning day of her long life of service, the women gathered in Oklahoma City were aware of something different about this young woman. Kathleen was clearly more than a glowing face surrounded by brown curls and wearing a flowing yellow dress. There was an aura of spiritual depth that emanated from her as she spoke in that lovely, rich voice with the charming Southern accent, the tone deep but clear and audible. One woman reported to the members back in her home state that the audience had never felt so much the presence of God. It was a signal event.

Kathleen felt especially blessed to be able to call on the wise counsel of Fannie Heck with the many questions and concerns she encountered in the first few months in her new position. Their goals and vision for Woman's Missionary Union marched closely together, and Kathleen recognized her good fortune in sitting at the feet of WMU's great visionary. Fannie Heck's remarkable gift of vision helped Kathleen to understand the long view of the Union's goals and helped shape her own plans to help implement those goals.

WMU's two gracious leaders complemented each other. Fannie was fragile in body and fifty years old, having just gone through months of recovering from cancer surgery, yet stronger than ever in spiritual depth. The other was just thirty-three, but had quickly proven herself both capable and winsome. In later months as the two women met to plan and pray, they realized that not only did they share a mutual love for the organization that was their life's work, but each had also lost a loved one to tuberculosis, a loss that influenced the future direction of both of their lives.

On the train returning to Alabama to prepare for the new life's venture before her, Kathleen methodically began considering what lay just ahead. It brought a pang to her heart to deal with the reality of Selma and home being hundreds of miles away, and a work and travel schedule that guaranteed precious little time to see her dear ones. Louisa and Hugh reassured her, declaring their realization of the sacrifice that was hers. It meant *their* sacrifice as well; this daughter was such an essential part of their lives, but they knew that when duty called, their child would answer. Had she not learned that lesson at their knees?

Kathleen began her monumental thirty-six years as WMU's leader by learning on the job *about* the new calling. Kathleen was determined to equip herself for effective leadership. So, armed with the brand-new WMU yearbook, she began traveling state to state, meeting with leaders, speaking at meetings and conferences, and learning from the grassroots how WMU worked in each state. Even as she was listening and learning, Kathleen was leaving bright beams of enthusiasm and encouragement in her wake. She was the proverbial "shot in the arm" to countless women who had been struggling, but who now felt a new surge of hope and commitment.

After one last poignant visit home, her parents saw her off to Baltimore, their blessings ringing in her ears, as well as the memory of the tears none of them could keep from shedding. Kathleen's first "welcome" to her new responsibilities happened even before she reached Baltimore and her new office. She visited at the Home Mission Board in Atlanta and was confronted with heartfelt pleas for WMU to help with the Million Dollar Church Building Loan Fund. From there, she went to the Margaret Home in Greenville, South Carolina, where WMU maintained a home for the children of missionaries. Next stop was Richmond, Virginia, and meetings with the Foreign Mission Board staff. Here were more pleas: They were counting on WMU to promote and lead out in the Judson Centennial Fund, commemorating the first 100 years of foreign missions with the going of Ann and Adoniram Judson to Burma. As with the Home Board, Kathleen pledged her best efforts, and, in turn, pleaded with them to lead her in the right direction as she began this new work.

Kathleen immediately wrote to Dr. Willingham of the Foreign Board to thank him for the time spent in his Richmond office and to say, "I shall try to keep constantly in mind the advice you gave me, and when I seem be going slowest, I shall try to be planning best … I shall depend greatly upon you and upon your promise to warn me when I am near the danger line." With her usual open mind and willing heart, Kathleen was building ties with convention leadership, ties that paid dividends through all her long and sterling tenure.

More than one dignified and fatherly board leader could be forgiven for having grave concerns about the ability of this petite, young, inexperienced woman to lead thousands of older women in their missions efforts. Most of them quickly realized they need have no worries. She was not an experienced, and somewhat formidable, power like Annie Armstrong — but she was every bit as capable and courageous. A number of national leaders of the convention were quickly reassured by one of their own, Dr. James Frost, their chief executive at the Sunday School Board. He considered himself Miss Mallory's "father in the gospel." He would not refuse her anything in his power to grant, and so he told those leaders. Frost was keenly aware of God's hand on the life of this remarkable young woman.

September 1912 in Baltimore marked the beginning of the rest of Kathleen Mallory's life. The story of WMU for the next thirty-six years was synonymous with Kathleen Mallory's story. WMU was her life. Kathleen felt she knew a little about the wide scope of her new work, but its reality would have been overwhelming to a lesser soul. The thoughts of living again in Baltimore — with its lovely memories of college days, and even lovelier ones of her treasured time with Janney — were wonderful and sad all mixed together. Kathleen dreamily thought of opportunities to visit with old friends, hear some great symphony music again, and attend alumnae teas. Fine ambition, but reality brought precious little time for any of those. Fortunately, however, she was immediately invited to live in the Keller home, which became a blessed haven to the busy young executive. Having her friend May nearby was a boon.

And, as in college days, Kathleen was able to worship at her dear Eutaw Place church again. Never would she have thought, all those years long ago, that one day she would be working in the same office as had the legendary Annie Armstrong, and worshiping again with her at Eutaw Place Baptist Church. Miss Armstrong was in her sixties now and long retired, but still the teacher of that amazing class of many children.

Miss Annie had begun her task at WMU in 1888 with no office and no equipment. Now the headquarters building was just blocks from the most congested business district in Baltimore. Kathleen's office was on the first floor, and she worked at a large rolltop desk. Over the desk, she lovingly hung a picture of Willie Kelly, a daily reminder to pray for her dear friend in Shanghai.

Being Kathleen — with her love for color and flowers and beauty — she planted window boxes and wrote devotional messages about the tiny blossoms and how they turned to the light, and away from the darkness. She and Jesse, the janitor, formed a partnership in keeping her flowers healthy. One of her first purchases was a typewriter, with which she developed a love-hate relationship. The typewriter came with a manual of instructions. The awesome discipline of Kathleen kicked in, and always waiting until after office hours, she taught herself to type, considering that skill a necessary evil since her correspondence was voluminous. Long ago as a little girl practicing the piano, she had declared in exasperation, "Surely the Lord never intended me to be a virtuoso at the keys!" Now the young executive felt the same way about her typewriting skills. She decided those crazy keys had it in for her and refused to let her finish a mistake-free letter. This machine-and-writer partnership was not one made in heaven, of that Kathleen was sure.

Never a day passed that Kathleen did not thank God for the advice and guidance she received from Fannie Heck. Kathleen realized that Miss Heck was no longer a well woman, and she did not have reserves of strength. Nonetheless, she poured herself into mentoring and encouraging the fledgling corresponding secretary. This first year was an especially busy year, planning for the Jubilate. Miss Heck carried the brunt of the workload — not only all her regular responsibilities, but in addition, writing a history of WMU's first twenty-five years, crafting a WMU hymn, and speaking in many of the Jubilate celebrations in each state. Kathleen accompanied Miss Heck on a number of these trips, soaking in both inspiration and ideas from the great leader. After a few months, Kathleen made several of the meetings on her own, great preparation for thirty-five more such busy years.

In November, Kathleen went to Alabama for the state meeting, feeding her heart and spirit on the joy of being with her own Alabama ladies again and being inspired by the message of Dr. T.W. Ayers. He was Southern Baptists' first medical missionary to China, now home on furlough. Ayers pleaded for the women to fund the building of a hospital for the needy women of China in Laichow-fu, Pingtu, not far from the city of the legendary Lottie Moon. At noon of the last day, whispered conferences were occurring at the meeting, and at the conclusion of the final session, the announcement came:

> Whereas the work of the Alabama Missionary Union has received powerful impetus by the faithful and efficient service of our former and beloved corresponding secretary, we desire to express our love for her and for our Lord by erecting a hospital for women in Pingtu, China, and bestowing upon it the name of the Kathleen Mallory Hospital.

For stunned moments, Kathleen was speechless with amazement. Flashing before her eyes was surely the smiling face of her young Dr. Janney. Jessie Stakely, sitting next to her, leaned over, grasped her arm, and sternly whispered, "Now, don't cry!" The normally articulate Kathleen could only haltingly respond to such a signal honor. And, just months later, her own beloved church in Selma gave a love gift to erect a chapel adjoining the church. Surely her cup had never been so full.

Kathleen Mallory Hospital, Laichow-Fu, China, 1915

CHAPTER TEN

1912-1915

Seventeen years ago, Kathleen had gone to Baltimore as an eager young college student. This December day, as the train wheels moved rhythmically over the tracks headed to the same city, Kathleen was a welter of mixed emotions. She was no longer a college student. Now she was the director of Southwide Woman's Missionary Union and headed to her new office. What a wonderful and shocking surprise last week had held: learning that a hospital in China was to be built with her name on it. It was almost too much to absorb for the genuinely modest young executive. Mixed in with her joy at having been able to be in Alabama with her own state ladies was the thought that crept in:

This would be her first Christmas ever away from her family in Selma. She knew when taking the job that she would very seldom be able to spend much time at home. Nonetheless, understanding something in theory and experiencing it in reality were two different matters. Reality hurt.

Kathleen had been invited to live in the Keller home. She and her close college friend May Keller, who had recently lost her mother, were determined to work together at having a special Christmas no matter their circumstances. Kathleen bravely decorated her office windows with fresh evergreen wreaths, and when they could get some time on the weekends, she and May went shopping for loved ones. Kathleen concentrated on gifts to send home. Her favorite moment in the stores was choosing a present for her namesake little niece. For this child, she picked a soft white sweater and matching white furs for little Kathleen's baby doll.

Two days before Christmas, a heavy snow blanketed Baltimore as Kathleen worked hard preparing a special Christmas party. A boatload of immigrant children had recently come to Baltimore, and Kathleen had been helping on weekends with Miss Marie Buhlmaier, the faithful home missionary who worked with Baltimore's many needy immigrants. The little children's faces haunted Kathleen's tender heart, and she and May hosted a special Christmas party for the twenty-five children and their mothers. There was a tall tree with lights and decorations and presents for everyone. Kathleen and May bustled around serving hot chocolate and cake to the little ones, and their first Christmas in America forever remained a shining memory for each child.

Kathleen's first full year in office set the pace for thirty-five more such busy years. She traveled the length and width of Southern Baptist territory, covering at least 8,000 of those miles on railway cars. Steam locomotives were not known for their comfort — an abundance of ash and cinders wafted from the tender box, and train cars were often too cold or too hot, but, nevertheless, Kathleen endured the discomfort with stoicism. She wrote to Fannie Heck about one trip: "This is *literally* a slow train in Arkansas! It has taken fourteen and one-half hours to go 265 miles." Even though the traveling was often quite daunting, Kathleen considered it a special privilege to be able to travel on behalf of missions. It was Jubilate time in WMU (the twenty-fifth anniversary), and Kathleen traveled many miles attending each state's celebrations. She wrote after a meeting in Charlotte, "A crisp lavender and pink morning set the pulses to bounding on Jubilate day and to rejoice needed no command — joy rose in the heart and ran over in songs of praise."

So much of the preparation and planning for the commemoration of twenty-five years of WMU inevitably fell on Fannie Heck's increasingly frail shoulders, but she was truly thankful for the young and energetic Kathleen Mallory, who helped with speaking, planning and implementing much of the celebration. The kick-off to a year of celebration began at the St. Louis annual meeting in 1913, and then each state held its own special events. Fannie Heck somehow managed time to write the first-ever history of the Union, which was widely celebrated in St. Louis in May. Kathleen looked on in amazement as Miss Heck called on all those who had been present at the organizational meeting of

WMU in Richmond in 1888 to please rise to their feet. Scattered across the vast meeting hall, only four women stood to join Fannie. Those women, in turn, looked around on the hundreds gathered around them and smiled to think of the glowing *future* of their beloved Union.

The Judson Centennial Fund was in full swing by this time, and the Jubilate was a strategic time to bring in funds. The gifts of the Jubilate effort went beyond $81,000, a magnificent sum in that day. Kathleen was thrilled to learn that Mrs. J.S. Carroll of Alabama gave $30,000 of that amount. The beauty of the effort, however, was the way it marked the beginning of sustained giving that indicated a trend in years to come. The Jubilate itself saw several firsts for the Union: the publishing of WMU's first history, written by Fannie Heck; and the adoption of a permanent emblem and a permanent hymn, also written by Heck. This was also the year that Girl's Auxiliary became a separate organization. Girls ages twelve to sixteen had been informally meeting as "Junior" auxiliaries for years, but now they were officially their own entity. Furthermore, 1913 saw another significant change: For the first time ever, WMU reported directly to the SBC; their voice was now heard.

For Fannie Heck, the Jubilate was a remarkably fulfilling experience. She had often talked with Kathleen about the shaky beginnings in 1888 in Richmond, with thirty-two delegates from ten states in the basement of Broadstreet Methodist church. And on this day — here they stood in this vast auditorium looking out over a sea of more than a thousand women from many states, singing with joy the hymn Fannie had written: "Come, Women,

Wide Proclaim, Life Through Your Saviour Slain." In her annual message, Fannie — WMU's great visionary — made a prophecy about the marvelous growth that would come in the ensuing years. Kathleen sat listening to the spell-binding words, stirred to her core and at the same time keenly aware that she would necessarily be responsible for leading women into that challenging future. Kathleen then led the assembled women in the reading of the Bible, using the precious copy given her by Grandmother Moore and reading from Psalm 11, Philippians 4:4-7 and Revelation 5:6-14, the song of the Lamb — rejoicing around the throne forever. Back in her room that night, she wrote on the flyleaf of her Bible: "Read by Kathleen Mallory at the convention in St. Louis, 1913."

May 1914 in Nashville provided a beautiful sight as the two lovely leaders of Woman's Missionary Union sat on the platform at the annual meeting in Nashville, one with striking silver hair, the younger with hair quickly trending in the direction of white. Kathleen loved to gesture to her hair and smilingly note the contribution serving in WMU leadership was making to its change of color. Neither leader could have known that this was the last time the two would be on the stage of the annual meeting together. In Fannie's inspiring message, "Facing a Prophecy," she laid out an ambitious plan for continued growth. Her gift for sharing a vision immediately inspired those who listened. The flagship magazine, *Our Mission Fields,* became *Royal Service,* and serving as its editor soon became a large part of Kathleen Mallory's working life for more than two decades. The Union's magazine went from being a quarterly publication at twenty cents a year to a thirty-two-page illustrated magazine with an annual subscription rate of twenty-five cents.

But all too soon, the unimaginable happened. Out of nowhere one Sunday morning in June, Fannie Heck was struck with agonizing pain. Within a matter of days, she was in the special Hygeia Hospital for Women in Richmond, and all too quickly came the diagnosis: cancer, with no known treatment that would help. Immediately, Fannie sent word to Kathleen, and there began a stream of cards and letters that did not end for all those pain-ridden fourteen final months. Fannie asked the doctors to do what they could for her pain, but not enough that it would sedate her; she was determined to write. Equally strong was her determination to never let a word of complaint leave her room. She dubbed it "The Room of the Blue Sky," and, true to her word, she refused to complain. Kathleen was in awe of Fannie's remarkable fortitude and courage. Each day, without fail, Fannie received a note or letter from Kathleen. She shared WMU news, little happenings around headquarters, family events from Selma and small tidbits that she felt would bring a smile to Fannie's heart.

Fannie saved every message, loving the way Kathleen brought her into the work of the Union through her notes. She smiled to read, "We made pictures today. The janitor posed beside twenty bags of *Royal Service* ready for mailing." Another day she wrote, "Miss Tyler and I enjoyed attending the conferences on college work. She was a lovely traveling friend." When Kathleen's brother James married, she wrote Fannie, "My baby brother married this week. I have never met the girl, but they say she is lovely." Occasionally, Kathleen wrote of a rare moment of relaxation: "Last night, I sat by the fire and sewed to my heart's content.

There is hardly anything which I would rather do than to mend or alter." Much of the time she wrote to Fannie about the beauty of everyday life, as "Did you see that moon last night?" One day she commented, "Every day seemed more beautiful than the last." Often a touch of nostalgia crept in; Fannie could personally relate to that emotion. Kathleen wrote, "Last night we had beaten biscuits. Almost as good as Mother's! They reminded me gratefully of the delicious ones I had in your hospitable home." Kathleen had felt so privileged to be a guest in Fannie's Raleigh home the year she began her work and longed for Fannie to recall brighter days.

In January 1915, which turned out to be Fannie's last January, Kathleen made a train trip to Richmond. By now the closest of friends, the two shared so many common bonds, and each felt for the other both great love and deep respect. Kathleen's heart nearly failed within her to think of carrying the load of leadership without the guiding star named Fannie. Not all their time together was spent in the deep pleasure of quiet time with a dear friend, for within each dwelled a growing awareness of what lay ahead. Fannie, knowing better than anyone that her days on earth were limited, out of her own depth of experience, quietly passed on ideas and suggestions that might ease Kathleen's way and enhance the work.

Fannie went into depth explaining how, in the earliest days, Annie Armstrong had strong relationships with the men leading the Home and Foreign Mission Boards. Being an auxiliary and not an agency meant that WMU did not personally have a "voice" in convention work and was dependent on the goodwill of the men in leadership. Fannie felt that at present there was not a particular man in the Southern Baptist Convention to whom she could go for confidential counsel. She told her young friend, "Kathleen, we need a few good men in the convention to whom we can go, men who appreciate our history and purposes, men who are alert to warn us against an unwise effort or inform us of any proposed plans of which we need to be aware in advance." Fannie grasped Kathleen's hand in hers, "I can think of several men who would be glad to be confidential friends of our Union if we would but ask it of them, Kathleen," and Fannie smiled faintly but sadly, "I cannot bring this about now. It is up to you. And I trust you implicitly." Naming seven leading men in Baptist life, Fannie smiled again and concluded, "My heart can rest easy, knowing you will follow God's leadership in this." Kathleen, gripping her hand in return, responded with eyes glistening with unshed tears, "My dear friend, my mentor, God will be our guide."

A sad Kathleen boarded the train in Richmond, headed back to Baltimore, her heart heavy with unshed tears of grief. One look at Fannie Heck's gaunt face told the story. She did not have long to live. Kathleen treasured in her heart Fannie's final messages and suggestions, pondering them in the weeks to come, all the while preparing for the annual meeting without the presence of WMU's beloved Fannie Heck. Kathleen already felt the weight of responsibility that must fall on her own slender shoulders. God being her helper, she would carry that weight. Her already intensive private prayer time became even longer and deeper as she sought divine strength.

May 1915 arrived, and with it the annual meeting of WMU in Houston. Throughout the long train trip, Kathleen prayed and prepared for the sad news she must convey to the Union; Miss Heck could not live much longer. When the afternoon session arrived — which was usually the time for the annual message of the national president — Kathleen rose and reported on her visit with their leader, emphasizing Fannie's deep faith in the future of WMU and her desire to challenge the women to gird themselves for the greater tasks ahead. Fannie Davis, longtime friend of Fannie Heck's and president of Texas WMU, came to read the message Fannie had sent for this day. As one, the hundreds of women quietly and reverently rose to their feet for the reading. (That message became the most quoted single piece of WMU literature in the history of the organization.) Fannie gave one loving challenge after another, including several courageous calls to service:

- See to it only, that you listen to His voice and follow only where Christ leads.
- Be prayerful in your planning.
- Be patient and persistent in your fulfillment.
- Plan not for the year but for the years.
- Endeavor to see the needs of the world from God's standpoint.
- Train the children for worldwide service.
- Think long thoughts.

Kathleen choked back the tears as challenge followed challenge from Fannie Heck's heart. The quiet tears traced a path down her cheeks, and she was doubly grateful for the fresh white hankie she always carried. The only thing to be heard in that vast auditorium was the sound of Fannie Davis's strong, resonant voice, sharing the message from Fannie Heck. Nor was there a dry eye. Those words ever after remained a sacred charge to every woman attending the annual meeting.

Even understanding the inevitable, the women of WMU refused to elect another leader. As long as she lived, Fannie Heck was their beloved president. Three months later — Wednesday night, August 25 — Kathleen heard a knock at the door. The telegraph deliveryman silently handed her an envelope. Fearing the inevitable, Kathleen opened the telegram to read the message. Mattie Heck stated that their Fannie had died that evening. Kathleen sank to her knees and wept in quiet anguish. The next morning, Kathleen sadly sent a telegram to Dr. Frost of the Sunday School Board, knowing she could trust her friend to get the word to all SBC leaders: "Miss Heck died last night. Funeral in Raleigh Tomorrow Afternoon. Kathleen Mallory." Thus ended the earthly life of WMU's great visionary leader, but Fannie's vision blazed on into another century and another millennium.

The year 1915 was one of loss and sorrow on more than one front for Kathleen. In June, her adored Grandmother Louisa died. Louisa's life had been long and fruitful, living until she was eighty-eight. Grandmother Moore had been a huge part of Kathleen's life and always very close to her heart, so her absence was sorrowful. Now for Kathleen, even greater challenges lay before her heavy heart. As she grieved her double loss, there immediately came to her mind the assurance of Philippians 3:13-14. Those verses became for her a call for renewed courage: "Forgetting those things which are behind and reaching forth unto those which are before, I press toward the mark for the prize of the high calling of God in Christ Jesus."

Kathleen Mallory Hospital in 2008 with visiting Alabama WMU women

Hugh Mallory: Kathleen's father

CHAPTER ELEVEN

1915-1917

With the wise counsel of Fannie Heck no longer available, Kathleen realized anew each day that she must even more depend upon God for guidance. She also understood that she needed to seek help from those who had the best interests of WMU at heart and would stand by to assist as needed. Consequently, Kathleen wrote to the first of those seven men who had been brought to her attention by Fannie. The letter went to Dr. James Frost, her beloved pastor friend and now head of the Sunday School Board. Kathleen asked that he serve as her "ears and voice" in the convention, knowing that she could rely on his advice as needed. She also promised to send copies of WMU's publications in order to keep him apprised of all they were doing.

Frost replied by return mail, assuring her of his willingness to assist as needed. He remained her stalwart mentor the remainder of his life. Kathleen's keen people skills stood her in good stead, and within short years, she had made fast friends of Southern Baptist leadership, many of whom privately referred to her as that "tiny little dynamo," but publicly, "that fine little businesswoman."

Fannie Heck's last bit of advice to Kathleen bore great fruit in the years that followed. In an era where women had precious little status in leadership, Kathleen carefully enlisted the needed support of key men in the convention to be her eyes and voice. The names Heck shared with her ring like a symphony of Southern Baptist leaders: the great L.R. Scarborough of Southwestern Baptist Theological Seminary; Frank Love of the Foreign Mission Board; B.D. Gray at the Home Mission Board; J.B. Gambrell of Texas; M.E. Dodd (who became known as the Father of the Cooperative Program); Dr. I.J. Van Ness, who succeeded her dear Dr. Frost; that great man of missions, Dr. W.O. Carver at Southern Baptist Theological `Seminary; and more. She began by asking one of the key leaders to speak for her as needed in certain business situations where a woman would likely be overlooked. However, Kathleen had to deal with her own doubts in one instance when she needed to turn down a business deal with a man. She first asked Dr. Van Ness to save her the embarrassment. Then, after wrestling with herself and praying mightily over the decision, she determined she would do it herself. And that she did.

Kathleen told a friend about the experience, explaining, "It seems to be easier for men to make explanations to men than it is for women to do so. Men are so incurably deferential to women that I never am sure that we women convince their minds, unless perhaps we are so unfortunate as to make an issue personal, and you know that women are naturally personal."

As Kathleen became more experienced and comfortable in her role, she learned to adjust to the way men did business. Her keen mind knew that, to be effective, WMU had to learn how to work with the male leadership of the convention. That was the route to effecting the maximum good with their devoted efforts. Over the years, Dr. Van Ness tried to help her adjust to the male mindset in regard to business. He commented to her that *she* liked to have more prayer and lengthy discussions, being sure everyone had a chance to express their opinions and ideas. On the other hand, he assured her, "I think perhaps you misunderstand the masculine, which comes to the forefront in our meetings … we come with the sense that our praying has already been done and that we must try then to exercise our mindset, even if it went against the grain."

The year following Fannie's death was a time of regrouping for Kathleen and the women who joined her in leadership. Even with so many projects underway, they sought to encourage the thousands of women who were mourning the loss of such a visionary leader. Kathleen became more conscious every day of her utter dependence on God's power in her life and her own need for even more time in prayer. Constantly, she sought to keep before the women of WMU their sole purpose — showing the world Christ's love.

More than ever, these high resolves were essential. Europe was at war, and it appeared ominously like America could not long keep from becoming embroiled in the conflict. An unremitting sense of unease and uncertainty permeated the very atmosphere of the country. Furthermore, close to home — and a challenge to WMU — was the debt hanging over both the Home Mission Board and the Foreign Mission Board. Dr. Love, the new president of the Foreign Mission Board, and the renowned denominational leader Dr. George W. Truett explained the situation to the women of the Union. At their presentation at the annual meeting, women began rising and making pledges of money and jewelry. One woman promised $5,000 as a thank offering for her husband, who (she felt certain) would give the money. At the end of the session, gifts and pledges went over $17,000. Shortly thereafter, Dr. Love called that meeting "the holiest hour we ever saw."

The women of WMU realized their need of a new president, and Virginia's Minnie James was their choice. Blue-eyed Minnie was a pastor's wife, brilliant and poised. She had headed up the important Jubilate committee, and the women were impressed with her leadership. People who knew her best commented that Minnie had "the mind of a man and the emotions of a woman." (Minnie ended up leading women magnificently for the next nine years, walking step in step with Kathleen Mallory.)

In spite of all the travel and responsibilities that were part of Kathleen's life — all the circles in which she moved, often with people of great note and standing in the denomination — her simplicity of lifestyle never changed. Coming from a privileged background, Kathleen could have been expected to be accustomed to a certain high standard of living. However, this was clearly not the case. She had never been extravagant, and certainly was not in her new role — although her appearance was always immaculate, and she always appreciated being complimented on a becoming dress or a striking hat. Kathleen was never without a crisp white hankie, and often smiled to herself to think of how frequently the ubiquitous handkerchief actually was put to use. She kept in style on the tiny clothing budget she permitted herself, often doing so by "recycling" a frock, bringing it up-to-date with a new collar or fresh trim. Sewing was therapy for Kathleen, making her think of home and Mother and the fireplace there in Selma with all the family around. She kept her wardrobe in order with the help of a friend in Baltimore who was a dressmaker. Her friend had a deft touch and a way of making a frock stylish. The dressmaker often smiled to herself at the fabric with which she worked, for Miss Mallory invariably chose some shade of blue.

Kathleen's amazing self-discipline extended to her office setting as well. Even as WMU was growing exponentially, the corresponding secretary used the same office chair and the same tiny desk and cardboard accessories. (She used them for over three decades.) Later, these moved with her from Baltimore to Birmingham. Just as she had in her state WMU office in Montgomery, Kathleen worked through one file at a time until her desk was cleared of that project. Then she moved to the next topic and methodically worked through that stack of files. Even when she had secretaries to help with the great volume of material and letters, she replied to hundreds of letters herself every month. Kathleen was so quick to respond to letters that her friend Lila Pye laughingly mourned, "Miss Mallory answers letters so promptly that you hardly drop one in a mailbox than the postman is at your door with the answer."

Among the multitude of needs and projects WMU worked on, the Woman's Training School in Louisville loomed large on the scene in 1916. Begun by WMU in 1907 and one of the chief projects with which Fannie Heck had been involved, the school had succeeded beyond expectations. They now had more students than room to accommodate. Dr. W.O. Carver, honored professor of missions at Southern Seminary, was a staunch advocate of missions education for women and its chief voice in convention circles. He was also an admirer of the talents and missions commitment of Kathleen Mallory: The two became a powerful team for missions advancement. He cast his considerable influence behind solving the space dilemma. The training school had outgrown it quarters, and the need for more space was critical. The WTS committee reported that $98,000 was needed for a new building. Kathleen smiled as she noted to the committee that "$98,000 doesn't sound quite as daunting as $100,000!" Brilliant Maud McLure was the beloved principal of WTS, and she agreed when Kathleen stated emphatically, "The Brethren simply must come to our aid." Maud and Kathleen were not only co-workers, but cousins as well, and the two shared a great love for the school and its purposes.

Now the question: how to get the support of the leaders of the convention? The normal procedure was for a man to present the WMU report to the convention at an evening session. How could this best be presented? Here again, the prescient visionary skills of Fannie Heck came to the fore. One of the men she had suggested Kathleen call on for assistance in the convention was Dr. B.D. Gray, head of the Home Mission Board. Wise choice. That godly man took a bold step. At the evening session in Asheville in May 1916, Dr. Gray rose to give his report and surprised the vast sanctuary full of delegates by announcing, "The first thirty minutes of my report this evening will be given to Woman's Missionary Union. May I present Miss Kathleen Mallory and Mrs. Maud McLure of the Woman's Training School."

Rather than speaking formally, Maud used slides to show the proposal for the much-needed building. Acting as if she were speaking of herself in the third person, Maud later told of the harrowing moments: "With shaking knees and pounding heart she very simply explained the rather crude, innocent slides as they were pictured on the screen, then sank into a chair to revive again." Next was Kathleen's turn to speak. Later, the *Christian Index* reported:

> As Miss Mallory stood before that great congregation in her dainty gown of white, I wondered if it occurred to her … that she was smashing a custom that was sixty-five years old and maybe more. I wondered as she made her graceful speech if it occurred to her that she was the first woman to speak to the Southern Baptist Convention?

And thus did 1916 mark a moment of departure — the beginning of a new sense of the importance of women in their work for missions. There were plenty of naysayers, of course. One dour-faced deacon informed Kathleen, "You are among those who rush in where angels fear to tread!" In her usual gracious manner, Kathleen responded with a kindly smile. For her part, the beauty of the Asheville meeting was the boost in aid for the Training School that resulted; she did not spend time considering the long-standing tradition that she had broken. And results were not long in coming. Checks came in, and among them one for $10,000 from the Sunday School Board signed by Dr. J.M. Frost, her lifelong friend. Women throughout the Union were elated when the cornerstone for "House Beautiful" (as the building for WTS was termed) was laid in 1917.

Whether she wished for it or not, one of the many tasks that fell to Kathleen was spearheading the raising of funds for numerous causes across the convention, as well as for specific WMU endeavors. She became increasingly adept at this responsibility that was laid at her feet. One special cause for which she made appeals was the Million Dollar Church Loan Fund launched by the Home Mission Board. WMU pledged nearly one-third of the total amount. "Pledge $500 to secure a memorial for some hero of the faith" was Kathleen's challenge to women. The HMB later published books picturing both the donors and the honorees of the fund. Kathleen drew a deep breath of satisfaction when she learned that more than half of those in the Hall of Fame were women, and the largest memorials listed were in honor of WMU leaders. In turn, the Home Mission Board, at the end of the campaign, acknowledged that the tremendous growth of the fund was due to the women of WMU more than anybody else.

The times continued to grow increasingly uneasy. By 1917, the specter of a world war loomed large over the United States, and unrest and uncertainty affected every part of society. Woman's

Missionary Union was no exception. For Kathleen, it meant more time literally on her knees in prayer for her nation and for wisdom to know how to lead women through the crisis that was sure to come. And, even as she sat preparing for the annual meeting to be held in New Orleans, the specter became reality. On April 6, the United States woke to the news that the nation had declared war on the Central Powers (led by Germany) and had joined forces with the Allies (led mainly by France and Great Britain). America was at war.

Fannie Heck Chapel, Woman's Training School, Louisville, Kentucky

CHAPTER TWELVE

1917-1918

Sunday morning, April 6, dawned, but its quiet tranquility was shattered by the frightening news: America was at war. Kathleen immediately went to her knees in prayer, pleading for her nation and for peace. She realized at once that this would impact the Union, and she must seek wisdom to guide WMU through perilous times. Change was not long in coming. The annual meeting in New Orleans hummed with news of war and of American boys going to Europe to the front. WMU sent a telegram of loyalty and sympathy to President Woodrow Wilson, pledging their daily prayers for the country's leaders, for soldiers and sailors, and, above all, for peace.

In spite of the shadow of war, women continued their many programs. Kathleen somehow managed to find time to write WMU's first-ever *Manual of W.M.U. Methods*. Her friend Alma Wright was one of the women who realized how much time the volume had taken Kathleen to research and compose. Kathleen confessed that she had needed to read fifty books in order to gather material for the project — this in addition to her already heavy schedule. Many a night she had stayed at her desk long after midnight in order to get the material prepared. Even as she traveled on the train, new ideas and phraseology would come to her, and she would scribble down a hasty note to be added to the text. Kathleen heaved a long, though inaudible, sigh of relief when she sent the precious little manuscript to the publishers. The manual contained all sorts of flexible plans women could adapt to their own societies and proved an invaluable help. Kathleen refused to put her name on the volume as its author, insisting that it was a compilation of the ideas and thoughts of many. The manual was a highlight of the New Orleans annual meeting — a meeting all abuzz with talk of war and those with sons and grandsons on the battlefront in Europe.

The women knew that all their efforts for the foreseeable future were going to be affected by the worldwide conflict. WMU, led by Lulie Wharton as personal service chairman, volunteered to assist the Red Cross. The biggest project involving thousands of women that year may have surprised some. It was knitting — mostly making socks for the troops. Fear was pervasive, and when news of troops dying came, sorrow was on every hand. One thing war did not change, however, was Kathleen's packed schedule. The traveling, speaking, writing, and directing office business did not slow down. With more to do, Kathleen could not help but realize she needed to pray even more; the work demanded fervent prayer. Often, she would remind women in various audiences that Christians were involved in spiritual warfare: "His is a progressive and ever-widening campaign of world conquest, and with him there can be no retrenchment."

Kathleen could knit with the best of them. In fact, she loved that she could actually be doing two things at once: She could pray while she knitted. Kathleen grinned to herself one afternoon as she came to the turning of the sock she was knitting for the troops. *Well,* she thought, *I can knit and pray at the same time — until I come to the heel. Then I have to stop and count stitches!* The war did not slow down the traveling whatsoever. She went from state to state, attending countless meetings and speaking so many times that she was sure everyone must have already heard what she was about to say. On a train trip to a distant state one fall afternoon, as she sat knitting and praying, a couple entered the back of the rail car. It was a good Baptist deacon and his wife. The gentleman stood up to put his wife's hatbox on the rack above, and his spouse looked further down the rail car and spied Kathleen Mallory sitting quietly, her head down and her lips moving. "Look!" she whispered to her husband, "See that sweet-faced lady sitting at the other end of the car? That is Miss Mallory! And, just look, she is praying. Isn't she a saint?" and the lady shook her head in amazement. Her husband, from his vantage point of standing, commented a bit wryly, "Fiddlesticks! I can see her from here, and she is knitting. I would suggest that she is counting her stitches!" "Well," his wife was not a bit daunted, "Think of it: She is making socks for the soldiers overseas — busy as she is, and all she has to do. I call that even more amazing!"

A too-full schedule did not prevent Kathleen from her regular letters to the homefolk — as she called Hugh and Louisa and all the brothers and sisters, as well as the ever-increasing number of nieces and nephews. Kathleen knew in her heart that the biggest sacrifice of her chosen service was the lack of time with those dearest to her. For a true homebody, too little time with family hurt. There was no one with whom she could confide like Mother and Father. She missed their dear presence and the feeling of being cherished and protected, even as they grew frailer and more prone to illness. Each time one wrote about a visit to the doctor or a particularly severe cold, she was reminded anew of the frailty of the human body. Kathleen also grieved that she was not nearby to ease their burdens and cheer their hearts. She did all she could in encouraging letters. Trips to Selma were few and far between, as the distance was too great. At the same time, Kathleen was doubly grateful to have thoughtful brothers and sisters who lovingly helped her parents.

The busier she got, the more she prayed. Kathleen's serenity, her poise, and her strength were all rooted in her prayer life. Talking to the Lord was as natural to her as talking to her father, Hugh. For Kathleen, to kneel was as natural as to breathe. In a message on prayer, she declared, "What Christian, advancing upon her knees in life's journey, has not felt the gain of spiritual strength even as the carpet has been worn away?" People who observed her life over a period of years began to realize that the secret of her phenomenal success as a leader of a vast organization of women was rooted in prayer. Outwardly, Kathleen was ever unflustered and calm, poised even in moments fraught with tension. Yet somehow, neither the grueling schedule she kept nor the pace she set showed in her face or demeanor. Kathleen's beauty never faded. Underneath the Kathleen that the world saw was a woman whose faith continued to deepen and flower. It became contagious.

Nothing gave Kathleen greater joy than Christmas in Selma. The first one she was able to spend with her dear ones after beginning her new role was unforgettable. Being able to be home was so rare that the excitement of it all made it difficult for Kathleen to fall asleep her first night back in her old room. The contentment and peace of home was a quiet joy that kept her awake far into the night. Home was a refuge and retreat for the tired, young executive. Here there were no pressures, just peace and serenity. Even the noisy chatter of a whole gaggle of little nieces and nephews was music to her weary spirit, a wonderful source of therapy and refreshing change of scenery. The little ones loved their "Artie" (Ar-tee'). Artie never forgot a birthday, young or old.

Kathleen's concern now was the increasing fragility of Louisa and Hugh. Her beloved parents were clearly slowing down, and what used to be so easy for them had now become difficult. They moved more slowly and suffered an increasing number of physical problems, yet the essential mother and father had changed not one whit. Kathleen experienced a pang of guilt that she could not be closer and take some of the everyday pressures off of their shoulders. It was just a situation she must accept. WMU was her calling, and her parents would have had it no other way. An occasional sadness in her expression revealed to a knowing eye that Kathleen was deeply concerned for her parents' health. Again, prayer was her refuge, and she spent long periods on her knees, interceding for them and their daily needs. Always, in stray moments, Kathleen's mind would go to Janney and what "might have been." By this time, however, it was a sweet sorrow, but one she had learned to deal with. His beloved face was always in a sacred corner of her heart.

As the war raged on, WMU's personal service chairman Lulie Wharton was hard at work. She went directly to Red Cross headquarters to offer WMU's assistance and to assure them the knitting was going on in full force. By mid-1918, WMU women reported making well in excess of 100,000 war relief articles, representing thousands of hours of knitting. Kathleen took a train to Hot Springs, Arkansas, for the annual meeting, wondering how wartime would affect their gathering. Minnie James was an amazing encourager, and when inevitable discouragements came, the president's serenity and faith bolstered Kathleen's spirits. None of her inner disquiet ever revealed itself on the gracious face that Kathleen Mallory presented to her dear women. The war did indeed affect the Hot Springs meeting, but it was nonetheless a positive and successful gathering. Attendance had dwindled to 693, but they were an enthusiastic band. Minnie James noted that every report of the Union showed an increase, and the women warmly applauded.

The entire body was energized by a special decision that came from their business session. Annie Armstrong had remained adamantly silent ever since her 1906 retirement. This year, however, Annie wrote suggesting that WMU name their annual Christmas offering for Lottie Moon. The suggestion was met with joy and enthusiasm by those nearly 700 women. (A few years later, Una Roberts Lawrence's *The Lottie Moon Story* was published, and the offering grew by leaps and bounds.)

Even as the women happily voted the Lottie Moon Christmas Offering into being, Kathleen's mind flew back to that letter from Lottie's co-worker Anna Hartwell that she had read to Alabama women and which God used to strike a chord in her own heart. That had just been ten years ago, but it seemed like a lifetime. It also crossed Kathleen's mind that Lottie would be mightily pleased at another vote that came out of the convention in Hot Springs: the convention (all men, of course) voted that women could be messengers to the Southern Baptist Convention. This had been a controversial topic since it was first broached in 1885.

That same month, the new residence at the Woman's Training School, "House Beautiful," became a wonderful reality. No one rejoiced more than Kathleen at the official opening, and her eyes filled with tears at the official dedication of the Fannie E.S. Heck Chapel, recalling how Fannie had poured her heart and energy into the school established to train women in missions. Fannie had been gone less than three years, but again, it seemed like a lifetime to Kathleen and the many women who loved her.

In June, Louisa Mallory grew quite ill, and Kathleen was gripped by a fear that her mother did not have long to live. Following hours on her knees in prayer, she made the decision to do her work for the summer from Selma, and accordingly boarded a train and headed to Louisa's side. With the aid of the telephone, good mail service, and efficient and dependable help in her Baltimore office, Kathleen was able to handle her workload. Her heart swelled with gratitude that she was able to have such precious hours with her cherished mother and thanked God each day that this was possible.

Then in October, Louisa began failing quite quickly, and, again, Kathleen gathered up her work and headed to Selma. The flu epidemic had hit the nation with devastating force in 1918, and Louisa's frail constitution was not able to fight off its effects. Kathleen was especially grateful for being able to be with her father at such a time, because Louisa's condition was crushing to him. And one unexpected blessing was to actually be with family to celebrate Armistice Day on November 11. However, Louisa was rapidly declining and had no reserves of strength. Each day, Kathleen saw sorrow written across Father's dear face. She would sit by the hour by her mother's bedside, and when Louisa had strength to talk, they would quietly reminisce over happy times together. When her mother drifted off to sleep, Kathleen would go to her room and weep in private, earnestly pray for strength, and then head back to her mother's bedside. On the morning of November 21, Kathleen and her father were sitting by Louisa's bed, Kathleen holding her mother's hand, when her mother smiled gently and closed her eyes as if to sleep. Kathleen soon noticed a quiet peace spread across her face as her spirit slipped into eternity. Hugh Mallory and Kathleen wept together over their loss, yet both were deeply thankful to have been with her in her home-going.

The following week, Kathleen gathered her resources about her, firmed her mouth with resolution, and returned to God's chosen job for her. There was work to do and a world that needed hope.

*WMU leaders attending a 75 Million Campaign
conference in Nashville, July 2-3, 1919*

CHAPTER THIRTEEN

1918-1920

athleen Mallory's awesome self-discipline was evident
in the months following the loss of her adored mother.
Thankfully, she was so busy that every day was full; this served
to keep her from dwelling on the sadness that crept in each day
when she woke. Every morning, Kathleen realized afresh that
never again could she talk with her mother, seek her advice, or
simply enjoy the blessing of quiet time together.

Armistice Day and the end of World War I marked the
beginning of new outreach for WMU, for out of world conflict
came a new awareness to WMU's membership of the needs of

women around the world. National WMUs had been organized in six other countries, including China, Japan, Italy and Africa. So many names and places were added to Kathleen's prayer list that she confessed to falling asleep sometimes at bedtime before getting to all of them in prayer. She declared, "Our joy is when our sisters from many lands join us in the warfare for righteousness." For world relief, WMU now got involved in "White Cross Work," making bandages, rolling gauzes, and making garments for the needy in many countries. Kathleen somehow found time to join in the White Cross efforts, and liked to think that some of those bandages might well go to the hospital in Laichow-Fu, China.

With the arrival of January 1919 came a sense of new challenges ahead, and Kathleen determinedly took them on. WMU had agreed to raise $3 million for the Education Commission of the SBC, with WMU being able to retain a portion of the amount for the Training School endowment fund. Then an even larger challenge loomed when the SBC met in Atlanta in May. James Gambrell, convention president, called for worldwide expansion. With both the WMU annual meeting and the convention coming on the heels of the armistice ending World War I, Baptists were infused with a sense of optimism and destiny. At the same 1919 meeting, the Foreign Mission Board asked the convention to consider surveying needy nations in Europe and the Near East with the idea of entering new fields. The board's dramatic presentation of needs led to a unanimous vote that launched the 75 Million Campaign. The challenge was to raise this amount in just five years. WMU agreed to raise $15 million of that, on one condition: the offerings for Home Missions and Foreign Missions would remain as they were and would not be counted as part of the total. Many among SBC leadership were not happy with this stipulation, but, knowing how terrific the women were at raising money, reluctantly agreed to allow the two special offerings to remain as they were.

WMU went to work, starting with the selection of Georgia WMU president Isa-Beall Neel as director of the campaign. Isa-Beall, a powerful speaker as well as a splendid administrator, wrote at the very beginning of the campaign: "It seems to me there is no place to be but on my knees." Women decided on nine o'clock each Monday to be a call to prayer for all Baptist women. WMU adopted the slogan: "Missions for the Master." Short months later, December 8, 1919, Isa-Beall sent a telegram to Kathleen: "WMU quota is over-subscribed by $3,000,000. Let Jesus Christ be praised." Of course, the campaign meant even more work than usual for Kathleen, which simply translated into still more rigid discipline of her time. In the first twelve months of the drive, she visited fourteen states, traveled over 21,000 miles and made 155 speeches.

For the convention as a whole, the campaign wound up as a disaster — but not for the women. WMU kept their word and gave *more* than their total quota. Some infighting and lack of cooperation doomed the efforts of the convention leaders, but WMU's tightly knit cooperative network remained on target, despite the severe economic recession that hit the nation late in 1920. In spite of the SBC not reaching its goal, lasting good did come from the campaign: During those five years, Baptists gave more than in the entire previous 74 years of the SBC. Furthermore, the campaign became the precursor of the Cooperative Program that followed hard on its heels. Not only that, but for the first time, women were named to a non-WMU convention committee: Kathleen and Minnie James were named to the Committee on Future Programs.

There was another stark financial difference between WMU and the various boards and agencies of the convention. It involved the salaries of their chief executives. Kathleen's salary was $1,000 when she was elected in 1912. That was only slightly over one-third of the salary of the Foreign Mission secretary. She would not accept more, and never agreed to a salary more than that of missionaries on the field. Kathleen finally agreed to compensation of $2,000 in 1920. For those who knew her well, Kathleen's wish for such a small salary was manifestly typical. Sheer self-discipline decreed that she would never live extravagantly. This was simply a way of life to Kathleen. She loved to give largely to causes near and far away, especially her church and all missions causes. Giving gave her great joy. Friends became well-acquainted with one of her favorite phrases: "Our giving should be fragrant with self-denial." Kathleen loved beautiful things but never coveted them. Furthermore, her simplicity of life extended to every part of every day. She could make a dress look fresh and stylish longer than any of her friends or family, and never did she appear dowdy or unkempt.

That same powerful determination helped her endure an endless but necessary chore: making detailed reports. Kathleen leaned back in her straight-backed chair one day in the office and wryly commented to her secretary, "Had Solomon been a corresponding secretary, I am sure he would have written a proverb like this: 'Of making many reports there is no end.'" The sheer volume of writing, speaking, teaching, and planning Kathleen accomplished would have vanquished a less self-controlled leader.

Kathleen would never have described herself as a person of charm or even of gaiety on occasion. Yet, those who knew her best noticed an underlying trait that never faded: her ability to enjoy and appreciate the simple and the beautiful, and to find beauty and loveliness in the most mundane and everyday kinds of events. There was a forever-freshness about her. Kathleen genuinely cared for others, but very seldom expressed her personal emotions to any except her family and her treasured friend Alma Wright. There was a special bond between the two, and on rare occasions when they had a free evening, they would have far-ranging discussions, including various personal concerns. The two often commented on how their minds seemed to move in unison on nearly every topic under the sun. In contrast, Kathleen's co-workers scarcely ever saw her display anything other than a cheerful, pleasant and businesslike manner. Most of them would have been surprised to realize that she personally did not view herself as did they. She once remarked in a rare candid moment, "I am so emotional. I have a hard time controlling my emotions." And she once confessed to Alma Wright's daughter, Annie, who was a favorite of hers, "I try not to draw upon your love more than I need."

Her parents, brothers and sisters also knew the inner Kathleen and realized her undying devotion to her beloved Janney, although it was seldom mentioned. As in most personal matters, Kathleen kept her deepest feelings locked closely in her heart. The WMU staff who worked with her felt like she had buried her heart with her young doctor and vowed never to love again. In actual fact, Kathleen was a true romantic and thought the love found in a true marriage of hearts and minds was the greatest of earthly joys. Consequently, she had never vowed to forever close off her heart. On the other hand, neither did Kathleen seek out such a relationship.

In 1919, Kathleen was forty years old, but even an astute observer would have guessed her at least ten years younger. There was ever a freshness and vitality about her. In one of her speeches, Kathleen, with a twinkle in her eyes, observed; "Being a woman you have heard or must hear it said, 'She's thirty-five if she's a day!' This simply means that she has passed out of the experimental stage into a fixity of habit and purpose." The women of the audience could smile with understanding at such a comment and appreciate the subtle sense of humor possessed by their leader.

About this time, several observant WMU leaders noticed at several SBC functions that Kathleen was seen in the company of the same attractive and highly eligible minister. Notably, none of them felt pushy enough to invade their Miss Mallory's privacy and ask about this interesting development. One particular evening, several women who were staying in the same hotel as Kathleen saw her come into the lobby wearing a striking white dress featuring a blue sash. One of the women drew in her breath and whispered, "She looks for all the world like an angel." And it was clear from the look on the face of Miss Mallory's escort that he agreed with the description. Another of the women commented, "Look, they must be going out to have dinner together," and each looked at each other, their eyebrows raised in smiling wonder.

This was not a one-time occurrence. Quite a number of times in the following two years, the two would be seen together. And yet, Kathleen discussed her personal relationships with none of the curious. Only her close family members and Alma Wright knew more of the story. Kathleen frankly admitted to herself that she was not sure of her own mind. Her warm and capacious heart genuinely enjoyed the companionship of her minister friend, and they shared all sorts of common interests and goals. Kathleen also recognized that it was not unusual for a forty-year-old single woman to think about life passing her by. She was dealing with reality; in all likelihood, she would never have a settled home of her own and children on whom to shower her love. On one quiet evening with Alma Wright, Kathleen confided, "Surely the sweetest joys of heaven are patterned after those of home." Alma was one of the very few with whom Kathleen felt she could bare her soul.

During those months of courtship, Kathleen felt a continuing sense of God's specific call on her life. That did not change. She also experienced a genuine peace in the realization that He was in control of her life and had led her to this specific task in leading women. On the other hand, Kathleen thoroughly enjoyed her time with her minister friend, their shared conversations and easy camaraderie. In the rare opportunities she had to visit with one of her sisters, she talked quite frankly about this new dilemma. Her siblings were of one voice: "Kathleen, take this seriously." How she wished Mother was still here so she could hear her wisdom. As always, Father was a gentle and tender support, listening with ears that truly heard and responding wisely in helping her think clearly and pray through what God would will in this crucial question.

Nonetheless, distance prevented her from much time with her adored father. His letters, however, were frequent and always encouraging. Even as she pondered this decision that would clearly impact her future direction, Kathleen realized all too clearly Hugh Mallory's frailty. With an ache for which she had no remedy, Kathleen regretted again and again the painful miles between Selma and Baltimore and how seldom she could see this central figure in her life. Thankfully, she was able to spend a week in Selma that Christmas.

Kathleen's nieces were excited when Christmas arrived, and "Artie" received a beautiful gold watch-bracelet from her minister friend. "Artie," was their unified advice, "you ought to get married!" In the inner quiet of her heart, Kathleen confessed to herself that she was almost persuaded. She began to reason inwardly, *Could I not serve the Lord and the Union devotedly as a pastor's wife? Minnie James did. Jessie Stakely did.* Never would there be another Janney in her life. Kathleen was brutally honest with herself, and yet, she reasoned, didn't Adoniram Judson, after the loss of his incomparable Ann, still enjoy the companionship of Sarah, and later, of Emily? On and on the reasons, to and fro, rolled around in her mind. Yet, the night came when, after long periods of prayer on her knees in supplication, wanting God's clear guidance, she knew her final decision. It was no.

The year 1919 brought some much-needed relief to Kathleen's heavy workload in the office in the form of young Ethel Winfield, Virginia WMU's young people's secretary. Minnie James had noted Ethel's dependability and skills, and, understanding the workload already on Kathleen Mallory, suggested she be added to the national staff. Ethel immediately began helping out in areas where Kathleen continued to have increasing responsibilities. The efficient young assistant stepped in to help in editing and management, proving a providential blessing to Kathleen and all of WMU for more than three decades. Ethel's ability to quietly take on jobs that relieved Kathleen of too many tasks at one time proved a true godsend.

Another new year was ushered in, and following a few precious days at home in Selma with her father and other family members, it was back to constant writing, editing, traveling and speaking for Kathleen. With the passing of each week, Kathleen's letters home became more frequent, and her home folks were keeping her abreast of Hugh Mallory's rapidly declining health. Even recognizing that it was inevitable her father could not live indefinitely did not perceptibly ease the great burden on her heart that she could not have more time with him.

In March, Kathleen was at the end of a speaking trip to Mississippi when she received the telegram telling her of her father's death. She headed straight to Alabama. During those miles on the train, unbidden tears slipped down her cheeks. Kathleen was grateful that no one was traveling with her, and she could grieve in comparative solitude. Reason told her of the great joy that her father was experiencing just now in heavenly realms — but her tears were for the loss of this one so dear, one who had *always* been such a necessary and blessed part of her life. She soon reached Selma and was engulfed in the arms of brothers and sisters who shared her loss and sorrow.

For the funeral of Hugh S.D. Mallory, all of the stores in town closed. Even the streetcars stopped running. The entire city of Selma mourned together for the loss of one so significant in their town, so admired and respected across the state. A small Alabama town paused in its activity to recognize the loss of a revered leader. For Kathleen, the wisdom of her father's words were forever sealed in her heart, to be taken out daily and remembered. As if it were yesterday, she could still hear him reminding her, "Daughter, always seek first the kingdom of God." Each day for the rest of her life, Kathleen could hear, echoing in her ears, Father's "seek His kingdom first."

Being more than busy was a special blessing to Kathleen following the loss of her father. Now both beloved parents were gone, those earthly ties forever missing. And now, in addition to a massive travel schedule of meetings and speaking, she assumed the editorship of *Royal Service,* a huge responsibility and one of great importance to WMU. The magazine was WMU's voice in the homes of Baptist women across the nation. Of course, Kathleen took it seriously, satisfied with nothing but her best. To her way of thinking, increased responsibility simply meant a need for more time in prayer. That astounding self-control, which forever characterized her nature, led Kathleen to understand that increased commitments demanded increased heavenly guidance. It was not at all unusual for her to fall asleep while on her knees. Kathleen realized better than most that the year ahead promised to hold still more changes for WMU, meaning more changes for her as well.

*Portrait of Kathleen Mallory during
her thirty-six-year tenure*

CHAPTER FOURTEEN

1920-1922

*K*athleen, she mused to herself, *what can you be thinking
of, to take on editorship of Royal Service on top of all
this travel and everything else?* As usual, Kathleen was riding the
Pullman train that pulled into Birmingham about breakfast time.
This way, she could arrive at the office in time to open for business
and lead employee devotions, one of her favorite moments of each
day. Taking on the editorship was important, she realized, and
she had prayed long and hard over the matter when asked by the
executive committee. Ever honest with herself, Kathleen felt she

was no writer — *but then,* she reasoned, *I can read and proof and get things done.* And already she had made use of travel time to go over hundreds of pages of writing. Baptist women around the nation depended on the compelling missions story of the denomination contained each month in its pages, and circulation was growing monthly. She felt a deep sense of responsibility when considering that there were already more than 43,000 subscribers, and she felt utterly dependent on God's guidance about content in the magazine.

Kathleen's new responsibility with *Royal Service* was simply one area of discussion at the annual meeting in Washington, D.C., in May 1920. Much of the meeting focused on personal service and the Union's work in goodwill centers. She and the executive committee rejoiced that they were partnering with the Home Mission Board in this work. Emma Leachman had been a city missionary in Louisville for two decades and worked with the settlement house that became the Baptist Goodwill Center. In 1920, the HMB assumed her salary and she was paid through the home missions offering that came from WMU. Kathleen was gratified with the cooperation taking place with the Home Board and felt it boded well in more combined efforts in years to come. Personal service was an effective part of WMU's overall ministries and unprecedented in Baptist work in the convention.

One of Kathleen's favorite responsibilities was making periodic visits to the training school in Louisville. The trips always gave her heart a lift as she found opportunities to visit one-on-one with a number of the young women there in training for Christian service, many of them hoping to go overseas as missionaries.

Each time she came, joining the students for a chapel service — or slipping into the Fannie Heck Chapel for quiet meditation when she got a few minutes — became the highlight of each trip. Memories of Fannie and her inimitable spirit were ever a balm to her own heart. Kathleen did not join the students for breakfast, but always arranged to have a little fruit for breakfast in her room. This gave her an opportunity to begin her day with a quiet prayer time, always necessary to the beginning of a new day of challenges.

On most occasions when she visited the training school, Kathleen spoke at chapel. The girls adored her and loved her unique style of speech, quickly aware that Miss Mallory never began a sentence with the personal pronoun "I." It was just not part of her makeup. They grew accustomed to hearing her begin her messages, "Happy am I," or sometimes, "Heartedly do I thank you." It was just another reflection of her deeply ingrained humility, as natural as breathing for her.

Kathleen made a conscious effort to sit at a different table each meal so she could visit with a different group of girls. One evening, a young woman at Kathleen's table made a comment that could be interpreted as having criticism in it. After uttering the words, the student could be seen squirming uncomfortably in her chair. As they stood to leave after the meal, the young woman came up and tapped Kathleen on the arm, saying, "Miss Mallory, I hope you didn't misunderstand my comment," looking at her with pleading eyes. Kathleen smiled graciously and replied, "Dear girl, don't bother about it a minute. I never let myself read an unpleasant meaning into what I see or hear." It was a salutary moment the young student never forgot.

On most trips to the training school, Kathleen had opportunities to talk with Dr. Carver and discuss worldwide missions needs with the famed professor who had come to be known as "the grand old man of missions," even before he was old. William Carver was an ardent supporter of women in service. He constantly advocated for the need to provide adequate training for women who had been called. Carver was also a great admirer of Kathleen Mallory and her deep commitment and missions passion. Kathleen had learned long after the fact that, back in 1911, Dr. Carver had been the person who initially brought Kathleen's name to the fore as an eminently wise choice as leader of WMU. Passing his recommendation on to Eliza Broadus, she in turn had contacted Fannie Heck, and the rest was history. The Carvers and Kathleen had become tightly knit friends in the ensuing years, sharing a deep commitment to missions.

When in the office in Baltimore, Kathleen would head home each night exhausted, but ever aware of all that still needed doing. A lot was churning in the Union this year. In fact, in February, the WMU executive committee had a meeting in Nashville to discuss the location of WMU's headquarters. Because the office had been in Baltimore for more than thirty years, the work had been dominated by one region. In the earliest years, Annie Armstrong and Baltimore women had been disproportionately represented in decision-making. The location of headquarters also impacted the choice of national leaders, all of them coming from southern and eastern states. There had been none from west of the Mississippi. At the Nashville executive committee meeting in February 1920, the Maryland local members were not present.

Members from Georgia and Alabama made a proposal that headquarters be moved. Thirteen of the seventeen states favored the move. A number of the women reasoned that the psychological center of WMU was too far removed from Baltimore and hindered the most effective use of personnel and inclusion of everyone in decisions. Of the several who opposed moving, their reasoning centered around the loss of money resulting from changing buildings, banks, printers, and even the charter.

Kathleen was not the only one to see how jarring such a move would be if sprung too quickly on WMU as a whole. At this point, her role was to listen, learn and guide as gently and wisely as she could. She also determined not to express a personal opinion, understanding that her voice might have too much influence. The names of four cities were suggested: Atlanta, Nashville, Birmingham and Memphis, and a good case could be made for each. There was a healthy realization among the committee members that this was going to be a shock to their constituency as a whole, so the women voted to defer a decision for a year.

A lot of major changes appeared to be in the making in 1921, and Kathleen resolved to deal with each as the demands came. She was excited about WMU's decision to employ a full-time young people's secretary, and Minnie James took on the task of interviewing prospective candidates, going to the training school in Louisville to talk with the top three candidates. Juliette Mather was the clear choice, and an inspired one she was. Juliette was a direct descendant of the famous colonial Mathers. The family was full of outstanding leaders, with two of her siblings serving as missionaries in the Far East. Juliette, a petite and winsome dynamo, did everything with alacrity — walking, talking, creatively thinking. Piercing chocolate-colored eyes topped by dark bouncy curls suited Juliette. When she attended the training school, Juliette talked with a representative of the Foreign Mission Board, indicating her desire to serve as a foreign missionary. The rather undiscerning representative dismissed her idea with a frank "You are too scrawny. You'd never make it." (What she *did* was serve twenty-eight years as a stellar young people's secretary, followed by nine years as editorial secretary, and crowned by ten years as a missionary teacher and publisher in Japan, Taiwan and Hong Kong.) The executive committee elected her in April, and the rest was history. Juliette Mather became one of Kathleen's closest personal friends, as well as a brilliant and valued co-worker.

The biggest challenge of 1921 was the relocation of WMU's headquarters. WMU's executive board pondered long and prayed much. It came to a vote at the annual meeting in Chattanooga. There were several reasons that the search narrowed down to Nashville or Birmingham. Nashville had several things going for it as the best location. The Baptist Sunday School Board was there and offered to provide offices for no charge. Birmingham was also appealing. The SBC Education Board had just recently set up offices there, and the board's secretary was the husband of Minnie James, national WMU president.

The official vote to move headquarters took place at the annual meeting in Chattanooga. Quite several felt it only fair that they not vote, including the officers who lived in Baltimore, plus Kathleen and Minnie James. When the vote was taken, the count was exactly even: 203 voted for Nashville, and 203 for Birmingham.

Kathleen sat in silence, listening to the vote count and silently praying as the discussions continued. Deciding it wouldn't be fair to ask Minnie James to vote, it was determined to request the treasurer and the newly elected young people's secretary to cast votes. Juliette was looking for a cue from senior leadership, and, understanding their personal, though unvoiced sentiments, cast her vote for Birmingham. Kathleen was thankful not to have been forced to cast a vote. The decision came quickly. The headquarters would henceforth be in Birmingham. At once there flashed into Kathleen's mind the poignant thought: *Now, after all these years, I am close to the home folk, but my dear mother and father are no longer there to visit.*

Several adjectives used to describe Kathleen in one newspaper's account of the meeting illustrated the impression she made on people, both those who knew her and those who merely observed. One of the reporters referred to WMU's leader as a "petite livewire." Kathleen just chuckled and shook her head when someone called the article to her attention, especially when her friend commented on the appropriateness for the description.

The new headquarters would be eight rooms in downtown Birmingham in the Jefferson County Bank Building (later the Comer Building). Quite impressive, in 1921 it was the tallest building in the South. Of the eight rooms, three were offices: Kathleen's, Ethel Winfield's, and Juliette's. The rest of the functions of national headquarters used the other five rooms. When Kathleen officially moved in, she happily brought her tiny desk with its cardboard accessories. And ever frugal, she never changed to another desk, keeping the same one until her retirement in 1948.

Kathleen arrived in Birmingham by train on September 9, 1921, descending the steps on the lookout for Juliette, who was to meet the train. As a friend later commented to her, "Instead of one little mortal, you were met by a whole delegation," for a train platform full of men and women were there to welcome her to Birmingham. Kathleen looked around in amazement to see a veritable army made up of both familiar and unfamiliar faces. Among the faces she immediately recognized was a dear friend from the training school and Minnie James standing beside her, smiling broadly. One person grabbed her suitcase, another her Corona typewriter, and she was introduced all around. Driven to see her new office quarters, Kathleen saw at once that indeed the Jefferson Building looked gigantic; it was easy to see why it was known as the tallest structure south of the Ohio River.

Kathleen's first Birmingham home was a boarding house on Tenth Avenue that sported a fresh coat of gleaming white paint. The landlady, Mrs. Dill, welcomed her graciously, and she and several friends escorted Kathleen up the stairs to her new rooms. She stood in the door, breathing in the fragrance of dozens of flower arrangements scattered around the room, along with a big bowl of fruit. Kathleen was beaming, her eyes bright with unshed tears. Flowers. There could be no more beautiful welcome to the city that was to be her home until retirement and after. That evening after the meal served to all the boarding house guests, Kathleen gathered the ones who were part of the WMU office staff together in her room and led them in prayer.

During all her years in Birmingham, whether in the boarding house or later in a small efficiency apartment, Kathleen's lifestyle scarcely varied. It was by now her ingrained habit to live simply. This way, *things* did not encumber her, and she had all that she needed. Never really having time to cook meant that she had the simplest of breakfasts, mainly consisting of fruit, and usually ate out at lunch, frequently at a cafeteria not far from the office. Kathleen was careful to budget her money and normally allowed herself sixty-five cents for lunch. Eating at the cafeteria meant she could choose her items specifically and not waste. She laughed one evening as she told the young neighbor who often rode the city bus with her, "Let me tell you what I saw today. I actually saw a woman *paying money* for ham and potato salad!"

A break for lunch was one of the few times Kathleen left her desk on the days she was not traveling out of town, although when visitors came to headquarters, Kathleen graciously showed them around, introducing the guests to the staff. The habits begun in her Montgomery office in 1909 continued throughout her many years as chief executive. The day would begin with files piled high on her desk, and with her incredible self-discipline, Kathleen would methodically work through them. She learned shortcuts that came in handy, like standardizing certain forms and regularly using familiar phrases. When something new came to the fore, then she applied creativity. If the pile on her desk was still daunting when closing time arrived, Kathleen would draw a deep breath, fill a satchel with work, and take the work home with her. Many a day she was the first to arrive, and the last to leave and lock the door late in the evening. Her friends and co-workers never ceased to be amazed at her sheer determination and unflustered and smiling demeanor. Only Kathleen realized the extent of her dependence on God for sustaining strength and courage.

Not only was the editorship of *Royal Service* on her slender shoulders, but also the editing, and much of the writing, of WMU's yearbook. Everything pointed to the need for still more help; each time Kathleen looked at her calendar and saw all the speaking engagements, she gave a little wince. She loved meeting women in all the states and sharing the missions message, but, at the same time, she was practical enough to know that efficiency could not produce more hours per day. She needed assistance to fill all the field engagements. Kathleen presented her need to the executive committee, and action wasn't long in coming. Blanche Sydnor White, a volunteer for China, had been employed by the Foreign Board for fourteen years. Blanche was elected as WMU's first field secretary in 1922 and was a highly effective speaker, traveling to many states and inspiring women everywhere. Blanche prepared for her new responsibility by studying all the minutes of WMU from the time it organized, so she started on her assignment highly knowledgeable. Kathleen breathed a sigh of relief for the assistance Blanche provided.

With Ethel Winfield to help with administrative duties, Blanch Sydnor White to assist in speaking engagements, and Juliette Mather to plan and implement all sorts of creative approaches with the youth, Kathleen at last allowed her mind to engage the wish she had nurtured for all the years since her work had begun: a trip to China and Japan to meet the missionaries on the front lines and see the needs of the world with her own eyes. Was it possible now to make such a cherished dream come true?

Kathleen Mallory with her father
Hugh at Ridgecrest

CHAPTER FIFTEEN

1922-1924

Her heart beating fast with exhilaration, Kathleen stood on the massive deck of the *SS President McKinley*. A hot August afternoon, flags were flying, the band was playing, and a cooling ocean breeze made the moment totally invigorating. Kathleen had anticipated this journey for so many years; now that the actual fruition of her dream was coming to pass, everything felt like a moment out of time. Was it really happening? She had found her stateroom filled with gifts of flowers, candy and fruit. Picking up a beautiful bouquet of red roses, she stopped to inhale their heady fragrance, and, unwilling to put them down just yet, returned to the deck so she could watch the *McKinley* set out to sea. For the last ten years, this dream had been an active one, beginning when the women of Alabama saw to the building of the Kathleen Mallory Hospital in Laichow-Fu, (Laizhou, Shan-dung) Province. Right after the hospital was opened, nurse Cynthia Miller sent Kathleen a personal invitation. Cynthia was the nurse who accompanied Lottie Moon when that frail and dying woman was carried aboard a ship in Tsingtao (Qingdau). Cynthia wrote: "I hope that sometime in the near future you will visit us in Laichow-Fu and see your namesake and what she is doing for Jesus in China. Now perhaps you had not thought of this, but won't you think about it, and let this glad dream of mine be realized? I believe it would mean so much to the work for you to see the fields in the Orient with your own eyes and then go back to stir the people at home." Kathleen had preserved that letter and often pulled it out and dreamed over it again and again. Now here Kathleen was, standing on the deck with her beautiful roses and surrounded by twenty eager missionaries headed for what would be their new field of service. The dream was becoming reality, and her eyes filled with glistening tears of gratitude.

As Kathleen related to her nieces when they accompanied her on the early stages of the trip to California, "Happy am I that I can leave with a mind at rest, knowing that plans are well on the way for a cooperative program plan for our beloved convention." Jacqueline and Kathleen had heard their dear Artie's unique sentence structure all their young lives and found that little quirk totally engaging. Artie told her nieces about the successful meeting in Kansas City when Minnie James had led the fruitful discussion about a plan for systematic and proportional giving by churches and individuals. WMU had been dreaming about such a cooperative plan. This May the convention had put feet to WMU's dream and appointed a very large committee to proceed with plans. WMU was a big part of the committee, beginning with Minnie James and Kathleen, plus a woman from each state with a WMU, making this the highest female representation ever achieved on a convention committee or board. Very aware that there were still all sorts of details to work through, Kathleen was nonetheless thankful that this lifeline for the convention was actually in process and right now she could rest her heart and enjoy every moment of the unique opportunity before her.

Thank you, dear Mother and Father, she breathed a silent prayer, *for making this trip a reality.* Her eyes swelled with unshed tears of gratitude at the thought of their making such a trip possible. Hugh and Louisa had left their Kathleen a handsome legacy, and with her usual devout sense of stewardship, she committed it to kingdom work. Pray God she could share the inspiration of this journey with women across the nation. The executive board had talked long and fruitlessly with Kathleen concerning her determination to take no salary while she was away. Knowing this trip would almost certainly be the only opportunity she would ever have to visit the fabled East, she was planning a trip of some nine months, refusing to receive a salary while she was away.

Again, Kathleen gave quiet thanks for the incredible staff assembled in the new office in Birmingham. Dear Ethel was a marvel, coordinating editing of *Royal Service,* dealing with office management, and generally supervising the various functions of WMU. Miss Winfield had been assisting Kathleen with correspondence, editing, and proofreading ever since she had joined the staff, and was already indispensable to her director as well as to the entire organization. Then Kathleen's mind moved to Blanche Sydnor White and the wonderful way she represented WMU in all the states, speaking with endless energy and enthusiasm. And whatever had Kathleen done before Juliette arrived as youth secretary? Not only was she a dear friend, but Juliette had already made herself invaluable as a remarkable leader of youth. Furthermore, her writing and editing skills were stellar. Juliette's instigation of *World Comrades* as the quarterly magazine for all youth organizations was an instant success. Now, with such dependable staff at home in Birmingham, Kathleen felt like the load of responsibility had shifted so that she could take full advantage of the long-dreamed-of trip lying before her.

There had already been the delight of traveling with her nieces, both of whom had never been far from home in Selma. The two nieces — Jacqueline, nineteen, and Kathleen, eighteen — adored their Artie, and were beyond thrilled to be able to accompany her by train as far as Chicago, where the three spent two days sightseeing, visiting museums and art galleries, and soaking up the uniqueness of travel with their treasured Artie.

Onboard the *McKinley,* Kathleen was a bundle of anticipation as Japan grew closer. Her fascination had begun during college as she studied literary descriptions of that mythical land. Then as a YWA leader, she had studied deeply and gained a truer understanding of the natural gentleness of Japanese women and their deeply tender love for children. Several friends in recent years recalled hearing her say, "If I could go as a foreign missionary, my field would be Japan." The first few days at sea were glorious, calm water of shades of azure and green, fantastic sunsets, and moonlight glistening on the water. How could anyone want more? Then on Saturday, September 1, a giant earthquake hit Japan. There was horrific damage and enormous waves for hundreds of miles. Kathleen soon learned that much of both Tokyo and Yokohama were destroyed, compounded by huge fires. Nearly 100,000 people were killed, more than that number wounded, and nearly 50,000 missing.

Ten days later, Kathleen's ship sailed into the harbor of Yokohama, but had to anchor three miles out. Then the *McKinley* moved on to Kobe, and Kathleen was finally able to go ashore in the land she had long loved. Its quaint beauty was all that she had envisioned, from flowers, to kimonos, to ancient temples with red roofs, fairy-tale curved bridges and lovely dwarfed trees. Yet, the intense beauty of Japan contrasted starkly with its desolation of soul. Watching people earnestly praying to gods that had no ears to hear and seeing lepers begging at the gate of the temple in Osaka gripped her heart. Above all that sorrowed her heart and the beauty that delighted it were the children. They captivated her with their soulful dark eyes and winning ways.

Highlights of the weeks in Japan were visits to Seinan Jo Gakuin, the Baptist school for girls. Kathleen felt a little thrill of joy as she thought how the sacrificial gifts of thousands of WMU women and young people in America had helped make this school a reality. She smiled as she left her shoes at the door, along with hundreds of pairs of wooden clogs. *How on earth could they ever figure out which ones were theirs,* she pondered. When all the women sang "O Zion Haste" in Japanese, she was thrilled to sing along in English. Kathleen concluded her matchless time in Japan with an overwhelming conviction that education was the best avenue for preaching the gospel there. She left knowing she was leaving the land that would forever retain a piece of her heart. And, of course, Kathleen being Kathleen, she first stopped to purchase little gifts for every member of the family and mail the package in time to reach Selma before Christmas. And, now — on to the mysterious Middle Kingdom.

In later years, the months in China seemed like a fairy-tale dream, with one glaring exception. The stark reality of the crying needs of the largest nation in the world were forever imprinted on her heart and spirit, and she was never the same again. The urgency of the need to share the good news deeply affected her. The nieces had asked, "Artie, will you see *all* of China?" Kathleen was soon convinced that one lifetime would not be long enough to see all of China and its teeming millions and their heart needs. As the ship sailed into the harbor of Tsingtao (Qingdau), Kathleen was already musing over how she could ever put into just a few articles in both *Royal Service* and *Home and Foreign Fields* all that she was going to see and feel in this remarkable land.

All about her were a cacophony of noise and impressions: junks plying the waters; sampans in the harbors; hundreds of coolies with queues bearing heavy loads in two buckets balanced on a long pole; shops filled with exquisite hand embroidery;

pagodas dotting the hillsides, picturesque but so sadly pagan; and everywhere, hundreds of women hobbling around on bound feet, never to take a step without pain from childhood on. In Peking (Beijing), she was astounded at sights in the inner "forbidden city" and the fabled Temple of Heaven, a beautiful but stark reminder of the lost-ness of China. There was so much to see and experience, and so little time in which to do it.

Traveling with Anna Hartwell up Taishan Mountain in a rope chair was unforgettable. There were 6,000 stone steps, but the carriers were swift and sure. At the top, she and missionary friends stood before the tablet honoring Kung Fu Dz (Confucius), China's greatest philosopher, who was born near the area. It set Kathleen's heart beating faster to think of the deep needs of each person she saw, all of them lost without the truth of God's love. In North China, most of what she saw was the "old" of China, not its emergence into the twentieth century. Kathleen felt like she was living in a dream, to actually be jogging along in a rickshaw, traveling with Anna Hartwell, whose letter so many years ago had rung God's bell in Kathleen's heart. *Here I am*, she mused, *actually in China with Miss Hartwell herself, seeing a land and its needs.*

For a brief rest, the travelers sat on a stone ledge of a well in a Chinese courtyard, looking into an open doorway. The floor was of pounded earth, the bed a *kang* (a bed made of bricks). Seated on the *kang* (pronounced "kahng") and staring curiously at her was the old mother-in-law — and pressing around her, three daughters-in-law and a total of six children of varying ages. Kathleen gazed in wonder at noodles hanging on slanted wooden fences to dry, pigs and children running around freely in and out of the little thatched house. It was chilly in the autumn weather, and the little ones were in numbers of layers of clothing, each layer filthier than the one before. The fastidious and gracious lady from Selma tried in vain to summon up the fragrance of blooming violets fresh in the air but failed miserably.

Kathleen noticed one particular young daughter-in-law. It had been her misfortune to have given birth to a "worthless girl child" (sadly, not a robust boy). Moving in Kathleen's direction, the young mother hobbled closer and then closer again, the little girl clinging to her garment. Anna Hartwell whispered in English to Kathleen, "Since they have been listening to the 'Bible woman,' she is no longer the household drudge." Kathleen's heart was wrung with pity, and she laid her hand on the head of the little girl, who reached out a tentative little finger to touch the strange white face of the beautiful foreign lady. And, even as Kathleen sat there, the young mother heard the message of hope from the "Bible woman" who had accompanied them on this visit to the village. The scene was forever imprinted on Kathleen's mind, reminding her of the hope that reached the remote villages of China through the care and sacrifice of missionaries who carried the good news that changed lives. The scene was replicated thousands of times, not just in China but in an increasing number of nations. This, Kathleen reflected, was why WMU did what it did.

Nothing was more thrilling than arriving in Laichow-Fu and seeing firsthand the Kathleen Mallory Hospital. She had to weep tears of gratitude that she could actually stand there and drink in the sight. And, in the nearby city of Hwangshien (Huangcheng), she visited the Baptist high school and college. A seminary and training school were also thriving, along with the oldest Southern Baptist hospital on any field. In the same city, Kathleen beamed as she entered the church built by gifts from Georgia WMU, wishing that every Georgia WMU member could be standing there with her.

Kathleen kept having so many exhilarating experiences that she realized there was no way to choose just one high golden moment. There were so many of them. What could exceed the joy of attending a meeting of the China Woman's Missionary Union in the huge city of Chengchow (Chengzhou) and hearing those many women gladly singing Fannie Heck's hymn in Chinese. The phrase "Come clasping children's hands, Sisters from many lands" forever took on new meaning for her.

Kathleen's heart captured the spirit and inspiration left her by so many missionaries to China. She and Addie Cox in Kaifeng had several unforgettable days together, as she witnessed Addie trying valiantly to reach some of the many thousands in her area — just one lone but plucky little lady with a magnificent heart. Later, Kathleen observed a woman doctor trying singlehandedly to minister to hundreds of ill women and children. Over and again, she realized that Baptists' 500 missionaries were trying to reach 400 million souls. It was almost too much to take in.

Kathleen spent her final weeks in Shanghai with her beloved Alabama friend Willie Kelly. Willie lived at Rue Lafayette, the large missionary residence where many missionaries came and went. Could Kathleen ever have imagined such a privilege: days with Willie? The white-haired Willie was a veteran and spoke Chinese like one. An educator of repute, Willie — and the missionaries in this, China's largest city — amazed Kathleen, both with the overwhelming challenge facing them and their courage in meeting needs, at both the University of Shanghai (Baptist) and its feeder schools. Kathleen had long before sent her Lottie Moon offering to her home church months, but now gave all over again, joining her offering with that of the women of the old North Gate Church in Shanghai, one of China's oldest churches now being led by second-generation Chinese believers.

Leaving Willie and Shanghai was hard. One last stop, and then she must go home. The trip was already longer than originally planned. Kathleen reveled in the sights of old Canton and the flourishing Baptist work there, especially rejoicing over the strong Baptist schools: Pooi To for girls and Pooi Ching for boys, with their combined enrollment of 2,000. That meant 2,000 young souls learning the wonderful news of God's love. Her next stop was fabulous Hong Kong, the British stronghold. She even had time to slip in a trip to Macau and see the amazing St. Paul's façade. A typhoon had destroyed all of that towering cathedral, save the great stone façade. Atop its door, which had stood since the typhoon hit a century before, gleamed a white cross. Kathleen stood there humming to herself: "In the cross of Christ I glory, Towering o'er the wrecks of time."

Immediately, the hymn made her think of the heroic Henrietta Hall Shuck, Baptists' first woman missionary to China, who had helped establish the first church in Macau nearly a hundred years earlier. Henrietta died at the tender age of twenty-seven with the birth of her fifth child, but, in her short eleven years of service, she helped to change a nation forever. A few days later, Kathleen stood at Henrietta's grave in Hong Kong, shedding quiet tears over the faith and sacrifice of one who had loved so deeply. Kathleen concluded her own China journal with words from Henrietta's personal journal, written just days before she died: "What is there below heaven worth living for but to serve the Lord?!" And, with the powerful memory indelibly printed in her heart, Kathleen headed home. She had work to do.

Kathleen Mallory riding in a rickshaw in interior China in 1923

CHAPTER SIXTEEN

1924-1928

Upon her return from China, Kathleen's mind was a teeming kaleidoscope of impressions and stored-up moments of not only great joy and exultation but also recollections of stark horror at having confronted the reality of world needs. "If some good Muse will help me," she wrote to the readers of *Royal Service*, "I want to incorporate into book form the impressions of my 'Orientating trip.' To the memory of my father and mother, whose legacy is making the trip possible, I will dedicate the book, if it seems at all worthy of their devoted interest in missions." Unfortunately, Kathleen never found the time to put all her impressions on paper. What she *did* manage to do, with great skill and passion, was share with WMU the new vision in her heart of a world crying out for help. In the months and years following her epic journey, she inspired an entire generation of youth and women (as well as men) with the commission to go and tell as she spoke all across the nation.

Kathleen landed in San Francisco more than ever resolved to promote the 75 Million Campaign. Her own eyes had seen missions money faithfully at work and being blessed and multiplied, making her increasingly committed to persuading women and young people to give with joy and to the point of sacrifice. When Kathleen left for her trip, over $92 million had been pledged. During the first year, money came in more rapidly than anticipated, meaning the boards could begin at once to enlarge the work both in America and overseas. Unforeseen by any of them, however, was the economic slump of 1921 and 1922, and the fallout that affected the rest of the decade.

Kathleen immediately began highlighting the importance of the tithe. Even giving 10 percent was a challenge to Baptists. As she spoke in meeting after meeting, Kathleen repeated a phrase until she felt like a recording machine: "Our contributions of money must be regulated by system and not inspired by spasm!" She kept her own 75 Million Campaign pledge card in her dresser drawer, and it lay there staring up at her a number of times each day. She looked upon that pledge as a sacred promise. Sharing the wonderful accounts of what her eyes had seen and her heart had experienced overseas became a crusade with her, even as Baptists had to borrow money to finance programs that were already established.

Shortly after her return from Asia, Kathleen enjoyed a rare weekend with family members when nieces Kathleen and Jacqueline made a trip to Birmingham to visit Artie and hear firsthand about her exciting adventures. The nieces were excited to see their Artie in her snug, efficiency living quarters at the La Salle Apartments. Marveling at how compact everything was, they looked at each other in wonder, recalling the large and spacious home in which their dear aunt had grown up. Artie seemed perfectly content with her simple lifestyle. The young women arrived to find Artie looking fresh and rested, not at all like she had just spent another exhausting week of work from early morning until late in the evening, even taking home what was unfinished in her office at the end of the day.

Kathleen and Jacqueline took seats, one in a small cricket chair, the other in a simple old-fashioned rocker. "Girls," Kathleen reminisced, "that rocker was the very one in which your grandmother used to sing her babies to sleep." The living room was spare, the floor brightened by a single blue and rose rag rug, and the windows hung with plain white organdy. Various pictures were dotted around the walls, and a few knickknacks sat on a small table, each with a story. Their smiling Artie related tales about the friends who had given her this item or that one. Both girls commented on the small daybed with its blue chambray spread. "I don't sleep there, girls," Kathleen beamed at the two. "Let me show you my snug little setup," and led the girls to the dressing room, where a Murphy bed was folded up in the wall. "Compact, isn't it?" Kathleen gave a little grin at seeing the wonderment on her nieces' faces.

She then walked to the other end of the room and pushed back sliding doors. The girls could see Artie's efficiency kitchen: stove, cabinet, sink, and refrigerator all built into one wall. The two could scarcely take it in, as Kathleen explained her daily habits. "You see," she confided, "I cook very little — for breakfast, mostly milk, dry cereal, fruit, or maybe a boiled egg. For supper it is usually about the same, or," she smiled, "I might eat a salad, or some spinach, or a sweet. I do love sweets!" The two nieces never forgot that weekend in Birmingham and the life lessons they learned from an aunt who was immeasurably dear to them.

Kathleen's trip to the Orient was over, but its memory remained forever bright in her heart. For now, it was back to work. At the annual meeting in Atlanta in May, Kathleen and WMU did what they always did so well: strike a positive note. When the figures were tallied the following year, the convention did not meet its pledges for the 75 Million Campaign. However, WMU *more* than met theirs. The faithful Lulie Wharton, WMU's first personal service chairman, resigned after eleven years, but stayed on another remarkable sixteen years as the Union's recording secretary. That summer, Juliette Mather dreamed, planned and engineered the first ever regularly sponsored Southwide Baptist event when YWAs met at Ridgecrest, North Carolina. (It became an annual camp and flourished for many years.)

Kathleen did not spend Christmas in Selma, for just before the holiday arrived, Alma Wright's husband, Carter, suddenly died. Immediately upon hearing the news, Kathleen wrote to her cherished friend, "I know that although you believe your dear one to be with the Lord in a place of eternal springtime, you must weep now for the anguish of renunciation; but in time God will wipe away the tears, and through this stewardship of sorrow you will come to love your Lord as never before." Kathleen packed editing work that she knew must be done to meet a deadline, locked her apartment door, and spent the week with Alma Wright. That golden gift of her time touched and blessed her friend as nothing else could have.

Minnie James presided at the Memphis meeting in 1925 and announced that she would not be serving another year. The announcement surprised everyone and caught the nominating committee off-guard. Minnie and Kathleen had been a marvelous team for nine years, and Kathleen would miss her sorely, as would all of WMU.

Minnie confided to Kathleen that, in looking back over her years in service, she would always consider helping develop the Cooperative Program as her strongest accomplishment. Because of WMU's role in the establishment of the Cooperative Program, she and Kathleen became the first two women to serve on a committee of the Southern Baptist Convention. The two leaders agreed that this cooperative effort, flawed and struggling as it was, would be the lifeline of their debt-ridden denomination. WMU remained strongly opposed to having the two missions offerings (home and foreign) considered part of the Cooperative Program, although the men of the convention fought over this sticking point for years. First developed in 1924, the Cooperative Program got its name the next year in Memphis and became the lifeline that sustained Southern Baptists in the century to follow. Minnie felt she was leaving something of a legacy behind, and Kathleen wholeheartedly agreed. Nevertheless, Kathleen was going to sorely miss the gifted Minnie.

Meanwhile, the Union needed to elect a new leader in a matter of days. Kathleen observed the working of God in special ways during the subsequent days, as the nominating committee quickly agreed that their choice was Ethlene Cox of Tennessee. Young Ethlene Boone Cox, of First Baptist Church Memphis, had already caught Kathleen's eye as she served as chair of general arrangements for this meeting. Tall and elegant, Ethlene was Tennessee WMU president and a riveting speaker, with her beautiful carrying voice and remarkable speaking ability. Ethlene was shocked when the committee approached her, and she asked them to give her overnight to pray about the matter. Committee members and Kathleen also made it a matter of earnest petition. Following the evening session, Kathleen drew Ethlene aside. Looking earnestly into Ethlene's eyes and placing a gentle hand on her shoulder, Kathleen spoke in that rich, soft voice, "My dear, you may be assured I am going to be praying for this nomination as God's open door." The following morning, a sleepy but resolute Ethlene Cox agreed to the nomination, and for an amazing twenty-seven years led as national president and then as WMU's full-time treasurer.

Kathleen's heart stirred with joy at the 1927 annual meeting in Houston the next May, when Ethlene Cox gave her first annual message and artfully linked the unfinished tasks outlined by Minnie James the previous year with the plans going forward for the Ruby anniversary to come in 1928. Her clear, bell-like voice was captivating, and the women gathered there recognized in her a special gift. Ethlene clearly revealed her pioneer roots with her intrepid leadership during difficult times, and Kathleen gave thanks every day for such a splendid new co-worker. Ethlene's great-grandfather, Daniel Boone, would likewise have been intensely proud of his descendent.

Kathleen and WMU's new president spent many hours discussing the need for women to become more involved in personal service. Fannie Heck's revolutionary idea was taking time to catch root. In fact, Kathleen noted that just slightly over one-third of all societies were reporting personal service participation. "Ethlene, let's pray about this," she requested. Their combined petitions led to the selection of a personal service chairperson to direct the work, plus requesting each state to select a leader to help coordinate efforts. Una Roberts Lawrence was the choice for chair, and for many years led brilliantly in guiding women to feet-on-the- ground ministries, beginning by stressing personal evangelism. And in Una, Kathleen gained another special friend who shared her own deep concerns. Lawrence, a talented writer, used her pen to make a lasting impact not just in personal service with women, but on the entire Southern Baptist Convention.

Una was working on a special project that would make a genuine impact on WMU and all Baptists: applying her writing and research skills to telling the story of Lottie Moon. It became a labor of love, and many letters went back and forth between Una and Kathleen as the book progressed. In March and April 1926, Lawrence was polishing up the manuscript when she encountered a particular question to which she could find no perfect answer.

For all the years since Lottie Moon's death and the emergence of her name as a rallying point for missions giving, she was universally known as "Miss Lottie." Through her research, however, Una quickly discovered that when signing letters, Lottie nearly always signed her name as "Lotte." "What to do?" was the question Una posed to Kathleen. Back and forth the letters sailed. Even in such a small matter, the two collaborators decided to err on the side of simplicity and use the spelling familiar to most Baptists. Henceforth, Lotte became Lottie and has continued to inspire the generations to follow. *The Life of Lottie Moon* was published in 1927, and so great was its influence that the Lottie Moon Christmas offering grew exponentially. In Kathleen's heart, the principle of the love gift as being over and above the tithe was simply a way of life. In WMU, as in no other part of the convention, was this principle so clearly lived out.

Houston served as the launching pad for planning the ruby anniversary observance, highlighting forty years of women in missions. Kathleen breathed a contented sigh upon learning that Ethlene had selected Alma Wright to be chair of the committee of five. She knew of no woman in the entire Union who knew more about stewardship or was more dedicated to the stewardship of her own life. Since Alma's unexpected loss of her husband, she had unstintingly poured herself into ministry for others. To honor forty years as an organization, WMU set a goal of 40,000 new members and a 40 percent increase in young people's organizations. WMU now had eighteen months in which to reach their lofty goals.

As Kathleen and Ethlene worked tirelessly together for that

year and a half, the ruby anniversary sealed forever the deep and warm friendship that bound the leaders together. Much of the 1927 annual meeting in Louisville focused on working toward ruby anniversary goals. Alma Wright was constantly in touch with the Union's two leaders, working tirelessly to encourage Southwide women to enlist and expand.

May 1928 in Chattanooga further emphasized the work in progress toward the ruby anniversary goals to be culminated in 1929. Alma Wright, a teacher of elocution, was passionate as she spoke to the women about faithful stewardship. None of the hundreds assembled for the thirty-ninth annual meeting forgot her fervent plea for each woman in WMU to rise above "Lilliputian giving." Juliette Mather followed Alma Wright with her challenging new plan for "Forward Steps" for Girls Auxiliaries (now Girls in Action). Even Juliette was amazed to see how the new strategy paid dividends in inspiring young girls to kingdom service. The GA Recognition Services that grew out of Forward Steps became one of Kathleen's special joys, and she particularly relished being invited to challenge young girls at the services, inspiring them to still more spiritual aspirations.

WMU members looked to the idea of stepping forward themselves in new organizations, increased giving, and an increased voice in the convention. They were already the best givers and promoters in the convention, but with very little *say* in convention decisions. The failure of the convention itself to reach its giving goals during the 75 Million Campaign unquestionably contributed to the growing financial problems of the mission boards. Although the women of WMU were not personally responsible *for* those financial woes, they were committed to doing something about them. Leading the challenge to fight debt was Kathleen Mallory. She had heard an apt phrase from one state leader, and it became one of her themes. Emphatically stating how the women of WMU felt about debt, Kathleen declared: "Women hate the three 'Ds' — the Devil, Dirt, and Debt." Kathleen then steadfastly and heroically led the Union in taking effective action against the three corrosive "Ds."

*Kathleen Mallory leading a conference
at Ridgecrest*

CHAPTER SEVENTEEN

1928-1933

athleen stared in dismay at the letter before her. *Surely not!* Now the Home Mission Board was suffering the same fate as the Foreign Mission Board encountered just last year. This situation, however, was far worse. Foreign Board leaders discovered the previous year that the Board's treasurer had embezzled more than $100,000. The Board announced that this meant its missionaries would soon be called home. When Kathleen heard the announcement, she immediately contacted Minnie James and other leaders, and the women took action.

Kathleen asked women to designate the first $48,000 of the *next* Lottie Moon offering to pay for the return of forty missionaries to their fields, and promised the Foreign Board that WMU would guarantee those salaries for the coming years. Kathleen negotiated with the Foreign Board for four months before they agreed to WMU's proposal. After the offering came in, the Foreign Mission Board told WMU: "The offering has certainly saved us this year." And Kathleen spoke for WMU: "Certainly (the offerings) have the seal of time's approval."

Now this new letter arrived, describing the current situation at the Home Mission Board. It made the Foreign Board's debt look puny by comparison. The Home Board's treasurer had been embezzling for a long time, and they were now reeling under a $2 million debt. Kathleen once again called the women to action. This year, every penny of the special offering was to be spent on missionary support. That saved the day for missionaries on the field. Along with these crises, again and yet again, another push would come from the leaders of the Southern Baptist Convention to make the special offerings part of the Cooperative Program. And every time, the answer from WMU came back: No. Emphatically, no. Meanwhile, when the Union met in Chattanooga in 1928, the celebration of WMU's ruby anniversary began and continued through the year, with plans to complete it officially the following annual meeting. In spite of bailing out the debt-ridden boards by WMU, the women maintained a positive and united front throughout the historic year. Even they did not realize just how important that was going to be in one more year. Thankfully, by this point, women were at least recognized as messengers to the convention and not merely silent spectators. Such recognition had been a long time coming.

The summer provided Kathleen an unparalleled opportunity to combine time with friends and a refreshing break from her usual schedule. Even so, Kathleen smiled inwardly when she noted what she had packed for the trip to come: a pile of editing work, along with her clothes. Her adored young Kathleen namesake was now a new bride and living in Cleveland, so Kathleen first spent several days of uninterrupted joy with her niece. Alma Wright then met Kathleen there, and the two headed to Toronto for the Baptist World Alliance, where they joined 8,000 Baptists from around the world. Kathleen felt chills run down her spine to hear the roll call of the nations. She beamed with joy as Ethlene Boone Cox, representing the Woman's Missionary Union of the United States, captivated the vast audience with her compelling message delivered in her own inimitable style. Following the BWA, six other friends joined the ladies from Alabama, and Kathleen soaked in the excitement of viewing several of Canada's major cities. On her return trip, Kathleen paused reverently at the site of "the haystack prayer meeting" in Massachusetts, where missions in America had been born, and then visited Northfield and Luther Rice's birthplace. She felt like she was touching missions history.

Memphis the following May was the scene of the ruby anniversary culmination, featuring a spectacular pageant with 500 participating and more than 5,000 in attendance. At the conclusion of the pageant, Kathleen sat in awe of what God had accomplished in the past forty years with a movement that began with just a handful of brave women in Richmond. The ruby anniversary resulted in over 6,400 new organizations, bringing the total to more than 30,000.

And there was more excitement to come, for there would be a new occurrence at the convention meeting itself, and Kathleen thrilled in anticipation.

She always smiled inwardly as she recalled the 1916 convention in Asheville, when she and Maude McLure had been invited by B.D. Gray of the Home Mission Board to present the building needs of the Woman's Training School. Now, thirteen years later, history was about to be made. If nothing else, Kathleen looked upon this year in Memphis as divine providence. The 1928 Committee on WMU recommended that the current president of WMU, Ethlene Cox, be officially invited to address the convention at the conclusion of the fortieth anniversary year. Ever since Cox's stirring address at BWA, women had been clamoring for her to speak at the convention, and the invitation to speak was extended.

The concluding night arrived, and Kathleen's eyes sparkled with expectation. However, when the session opened, J.W. Porter from Kentucky brought a resolution from the Kentucky Baptist General Association protesting any woman addressing the SBC on the grounds that it was unscriptural. Porter declared: "Eve tempted Adam. Now the SBC is tempting women. The women would do all right if the petticoated preachers would leave them alone." Immediately, M.E. Dodd, pastor of Shreveport's First Baptist Church, responded: "In Christ there is neither male nor female. We are one in Christ." Thunderous applause greeted Dodd's response, and a veritable avalanche of "noes" sounded for Porter's resolution. Kathleen watched with an inward smile as

Porter immediately picked up his hat and walked out.

Renowned Baptist orator and president of the SBC, Dr. George W. Truett, was presiding. Both that night and in years to come, Ethlene Boone Cox became known as the only person in the same category of oratory as George W. Truett. They were in a class all their own. Tall and beautiful, poised and persuasive, Ethlene's musical voice clearly drove home her point: "No woman went to sleep in the garden. No women betrayed Him. It was the women who followed Him to Calvary and wept for Him. It was women who were at the tomb." The vast audience in Memphis sat transfixed. A reporter had just weeks earlier written after hearing her: "What a winsome personality is Mrs. Cox. She had a clear, musical voice that is easily carried to the utmost limits of any auditorium ... I was so spellbound that I found when she had finished her matchless address that I had only the most meager notes. I was so swept away with the power of her eloquence that ... I completely lost sight of the fact that I was supposed to be covering her address." Kathleen sat, her eyes glistening with gratified tears. It marked a special day for women in kingdom service, and she silently thanked God for such a blessing.

But a black cloud hovered just around the corner. October 24, 1929 was a day Kathleen would never forget. The nation came to a grinding halt when the stock market collapsed in spectacular fashion. For months, Kathleen had been making the economy a point of daily petition as she knelt and prayed long and hard over the downward slide of America's finances, deeply concerned about its effects on missionaries hard at work both in the homeland and in countries across the globe. Just this July, eleven new missionaries were appointed, most of them for China, but the Foreign Mission Board regretfully informed them they could not depart for the field — there was not enough money to send them. As soon as Kathleen and WMU's leaders heard the distressing news, they sprang into action and quickly contacted the Board, stating categorically that WMU would stand good for those salaries: Send the new missionaries. In August, Kathleen had the special joy of reading in the news that the SS *Empress of Asia* had sailed for China with seven new Baptist missionaries aboard.

But things rapidly deteriorated. It was the most colossal financial collapse in the stock market's 150-year history. The nation was blanketed in the despair of the Depression. On one hand, money was growing scarcer, even while bread and soup lines grew longer. Kathleen agonized in prayer each day, pleading for wisdom to know how to lead the Union in such insecure times, surely a challenge larger than any she had yet faced. The integrity of the Union was at stake, and her keen mind realized that there was no easy, overnight answer. This was going to require years of wisdom and careful planning. Immediately, Kathleen recognized that a positive note was the wise choice; therefore, women led the way for the entire convention in setting a positive tone, realizing full well that dwelling on gloom, despair and agony on end was not going to help solve anything. Instead, Kathleen noted at the annual meeting, "If the letters 'd, e, i' were removed from 'depression', the words 'press on' would remain."

Exactly as Kathleen had surmised on that fateful day in October, debt and financial problems consumed all the convention boards for the next several years while the country struggled to survive. WMU was the only Baptist entity that was not operating in the red. Kathleen added several "Ds" to the list that women detested as she talked of the weight of Baptist debt, even though it was not WMU's personal debt. Kathleen reminded women repeatedly that WMU detested "distasteful, deadening, disturbing, discouraging, distracting debts. And, as usual, women blazed the trail in doing something about it. The 1929 Lottie Moon offering returned sixty foreign missionaries to their fields, and in 1930, designated that funds be allocated for twenty new missionaries (fifteen of whom would be women). After the low point of the Depression in 1932, Kathleen rejoiced that the offering never again showed a loss. In point of fact, at the end of 1931, WMU offerings made up an amazing 70 percent of the Foreign Mission Board's income. (Two years later, Dr. Charles Maddry, the new FMB secretary, stated at the annual meeting, "The one thing that has saved our work from disaster and has enabled us to carry on at all has been the substantial and timely support given by the Woman's Missionary Union." Kathleen sat listening as silent tears of joy slid down her cheeks.)

Always on the alert to find a practical way to meet any looming crisis, Kathleen daily grew more aware of her utter dependency on prayer. In the fourth year of the Depression, when 25 percent of the nation was unemployed, Kathleen boldly led WMU to adopt a plan to reduce the debt of the FMB, suggesting that the SBC devise some plan for saving the convention and its agencies. After months of negotiations, including Kathleen and her women adamantly and repeatedly defending the two missions offerings from inclusion in the Cooperative Program, the convention adopted a plan called the Hundred Thousand Club. WMU agreed to support it and, as usual, became the stable mainstay that led to its successful conclusion. Occasionally, while sitting at her desk, Kathleen would allow a stray thought to drift through her mind: *Wouldn't Father be smiling to think of his classical scholar daughter embroiled in the daily nitty-gritty of finance, and actually doing a fairly decent job of it?* Kathleen made sure the new plan was front and center and began using a new stationery letterhead: *For a Debtless Denomination by 1945.* Of the $3 million needed for the convention, WMU accepted a pledge of $1 million. This, in spite of WMU membership making up only 13.3 percent of total SBC membership, was amazing. It amounted to a small minority supporting the majority of the work of missions. There was not a time as she prayed that Kathleen did not give thanks to God that the women of the Union had not one moment bowed to defeat.

Although the Depression affected every aspect of WMU's work, the Union continued strong, sometimes bending in the winds of adversity but never blown off course. Kathleen had personally never lived extravagantly, so practicing economy now came naturally. She lived in such a spartan, non-frivolous style that sometimes her staff would be surprised at a lighthearted comment or suggestion she would occasionally make. One day when a friend had sent a box of candy to a hard-working committee that labored around the conference table for long hours, Kathleen surprised them all when she smiled and spoke up abruptly, "Let's have some refreshments. I'm hungry." After the meeting, one young committee member murmured to her older counterpart, "I never thought of *Miss Mallory* being hungry."

Just short years earlier, a providential addition to the ranks of WMU leadership came with Ethlene Cox's selection of Una Roberts Lawrence of Missouri as personal service chairman. Kathleen and Una had collaborated frequently when Una was writing the biography of Lottie Moon, and Kathleen quickly developed a profound appreciation for Una's keen mind. Then in 1931, Lawrence took on the task of mission study chairman, and her writing skills and leadership qualities became invaluable to the Union. The Home Mission Board simultaneously employed her as mission study editor, and her talents impacted the entire convention.

One of Una Roberts Lawrence's greatest contributions remained unsung and mostly unnoticed. She was a trailblazer in friendship and cooperation with African-American women. Her personal relationship with the renowned Nannie Helen Burroughs, director of National Baptist Women, was built on mutual love and respect.

Blanche Sydnor White was another advocate for deepening the bonds between the two groups of Baptist women, and she, too, was a close friend of Nannie's. Those three were groundbreakers and shared an extraordinary friendship, truly remarkable in that era. Una and Blanche realized that to bridge the chasm between the two organizations of women, they needed the support and guidance of Kathleen Mallory. They also understood that their own backgrounds were at variance with Kathleen's in their views of race relations. Una had been raised in a border state and viewed America's history of slavery far differently than did Kathleen, a daughter of the Old South that she was. Quietly and lovingly, the two women set about working on developing ties between their Union's leader and their friend Nannie Burroughs.

Kathleen and Nannie Helen had been born the same year, yet their childhoods could scarcely have been more different. Kathleen grew up in Selma, entrenched in the traditions of two centuries of slavery that preceded a devastating war. Hugh and Louisa Mallory were kind, caring, and paternalistic in their dealings with the black population of Selma. They were highly respected by the black community, but nonetheless a great gulf was fixed between. Clearly, the view of race held by Una and Blanche was foreign to Kathleen's deeply ingrained way of thinking. Una and Blanche recognized this fact, and, respecting their leader so deeply, proceeded prayerfully and slowly.

Kathleen and all of the Union had been consumed by the challenges that the Depression had presented, so other issues had taken a back burner. The Depression affected not only the convention and WMU collectively — every person was impacted to some degree by the deprivations and struggles that were the inevitable side effects of economic standstill. Kathleen was shocked when she received a letter from Ethlene Cox early in 1933. She and Ethlene had made an inseparable team in leadership, working in beautiful harmony and blending of skills for eight years. Kathleen opened Ethlene's letter to read that her beloved husband, Wiley, had suffered deep financial losses and the strain of the past several years had led to crippling heart disease. His condition was now critical. Ethlene was on the horns of a dilemma: Wiley needed her physical presence to keep him going; however, she must now have an income. Yet, it was nearly unthinkable to leave the presidency of the Union she loved so dearly. Even so, Wiley's need left her no choice as she privately explained to Kathleen the choices she faced. There *was* no alternative. Wiley's need was desperate.

Sitting long moments, trying to absorb the implications of her friend's letter, Kathleen's mind began to whirl. Losing Ethlene Boone Cox as national president meant not only forfeiting a stellar planner and leader, it meant as well the painful loss of WMU's single most effective and inspirational spokesperson. Taking a deep breath, Kathleen proceeded to do what she always did when faced with a critical issue: She sank to her knees in prayer, beseeching God for divine guidance and courage in time of need.

Kathleen Mallory with Juliette
Mather and Ethlene Boone Cox
at Ridgecrest, WMU Week

CHAPTER EIGHTEEN

1933-1936

*O*nly through prayer could Kathleen rest her heart over the necessity of losing Ethlene Cox as president, finding she could rest in knowing of God's control and sovereignty. Most reluctantly, the nominating committee set to work to select the next president — and, a year later, Kathleen looked back and mentally shook her head at her own lack of faith. God had directed WMU to the very person to lead for this period, and, at the same time, provided the means for Ethlene to both care for her husband and remain extremely involved in helping the Union she so greatly loved.

Committee members did not meet until the annual meeting, but each began looking and praying about possibilities of a president to succeed Ethlene. Several thought of Laura Armstrong from Missouri. Daughter of a preacher, a teacher in her own right, wife of an attorney, and passionate about YWAs, Laura was a leader in stewardship and tithing promotion. "Laura D," as her father called her, became Missouri's first WMU president in 1923. And, when the Southern Baptist Convention broke with its long tradition and put two women on the powerful executive committee, Laura Armstrong was one of them.

The Union's choice of Laura proved to be an inspired one, although it was not easily reached. In fact, the nominating committee didn't meet until the annual meeting in Washington, D.C. Two names were before the committee: Laura, and the remarkable Alma Wright, a popular speaker and a long-time leader in the Union. Kathleen determined to express no opinion, for she did not want to influence anyone's choice — and knowing Alma as well as she did, and cherishing their close friendship, she could not feel it right to be part of the discussion. The committee had a custom it had followed for years: They would stand in a circle, join hands, and pray for God's choice to be revealed. Prior to that meeting, Alma Wright was present and asked that she *not* be considered. After the women prayed, as was their custom, secret ballots were used: Laura was the unanimous choice. And, so, WMU elected its first president from west of the Mississippi.

Laura was tall, always erect, a handsome woman. Her clothes were always perfectly fitted, her appearance reassuring. Following the "golden voice" of Ethlene Boone Cox was not easy for her. It would have been difficult for anyone. Laura's speech pattern was somewhat halting, although her voice was melodious and her content inspired. The years to come proved the steel in Laura Armstrong, and Kathleen smiled inwardly, yet again, at the way God always provided what His people needed. On the heels of Ethlene's reluctant resignation, Providence again went to work. The executive committee, who were already looking toward the Jubilee and celebrating fifty years of WMU, unanimously agreed to ask Ethlene, an accomplished writer, to prepare the history of WMU for the occasion. And Providence further provided, for as beloved long-time treasurer Elizabeth Lowndes retired the same year, the Union immediately requested Ethlene to become WMU's first full-time employed treasurer.

Ethlene contacted Kathleen at once to talk about the position. Treasurer? Ethlene was shocked. She knew words and she knew people, but she had never been interested in math. Kathleen had to talk long and persuasively to help Ethlene understand what an asset she would be, with her vast knowledge of WMU and its inner workings, of how the funds were used, and of where the greatest needs lay. Ethlene, determined to care for Wiley and at the same time devoted to the work of WMU, prayed along with Kathleen and hesitantly accepted the post. And as if ordained by heaven, this same month Mattie Morgan, a friend of Ethlene's from South Carolina, was passing through Memphis and stopped to visit with Ethlene for several days. The short visit turned into many years, for Mattie was trained in finances and eagerly offered to help her friend. Mattie began by training Ethlene in accounting techniques and ended up assisting her for years to come. This godsend enabled Ethlene to have time to meet the many speaking obligations coming to her from all over the nation. Kathleen gave thanks every day for the gift of the talents and input provided by Ethlene, who served multiple roles in the Union and was Kathleen's right hand. Ethlene was also deeply involved in the decision-making processes of the Union that, with the passing of the years, had become increasingly complex.

Kathleen was also grateful for their new, highly intelligent, and committed president, now part of WMU's leadership during times of such great distress in the country. Laura Armstrong came into office when the nation was struggling to pull out of the Depression. She first presided at the 1934 meeting in Fort Worth, and she and Kathleen were profoundly gratified that Annie Armstrong finally allowed her name to be given to the home missions offering at Easter time. When Kathleen stood, and, in her rich and measured voice, shared the news with the women, a happy murmur of surprise and satisfaction made its way through the auditorium. Annie had not been easily persuaded and only agreed when friends convinced her that such a change would mean the giving would increase. And increase it did.

Kathleen noticed that with the passing of the years, she had an increasing proclivity for thinking back over years gone by. She would note choices she had made and experiences she had been through that had profoundly influenced her personally as well as impacted her beloved Union. One beautiful bright spot in the trying years of the Depression was the spiritual high of her summer in South America in 1930. Just as with her trip to the Orient, Kathleen paid her own way and considered this as a working trip. She now absorbed the needs and flavor of another part of the world. However, the first few days out of New York made her queasily wonder if she would *live* to reach her destination, for the ship encountered a violent storm. For two and a half days, she lay in her berth, spending most of the time groaning. The English stewardess attempted to console her: "Several sailors are sick, too. So are the musicians, and even one of the waiters is ill!" Kathleen looked up with dull eyes and tried to muster a smile: "Indeed? I am sorry for their discomfort, but beyond that I just don't care! Music would be maddening, and dining room service is useless right now! If only *all* the sailors were sick, do you think the boat might stop?"

The seas did calm, and Kathleen had the special joy of celebrating daily devotions with the great George W. Truett and his wife. The Truetts were headed to Brazil for evangelistic services, and Una Roberts Lawrence, soon to become the first mission study leader for the SBC, was headed to South America for research and inspiration for a mission study book. It marked the beginning of a close friendship between the two women who became firm coworkers for the rest of their lives. When Dr. Truett led devotions for them each day, he always used the WMU prayer calendar.

Brazil was Kathleen's first country to visit on this trip, and the profusion of wonderful flowers filled her senses. She was amazed to find orchids in Brazil as plentiful as goldenrod in Alabama.

There were massive cathedrals all over the city of Rio, and yet vast areas of slums and dire poverty. The image that most pierced her heart was the abundance of crosses everywhere she looked — massive crosses, small crosses, wooden crosses, gold crosses. And, in most places, they were merely a symbol — a symbol with no real meaning. It cut the heart. She found it as meaningless in the way the cross was used in Brazil as she had found the images of Buddha in China. The cross still standing on St. Paul's façade in Macau had been a symbol of triumph. Here in Brazil, however, the cross often had no meaning.

But, Kathleen recalled, as she reminisced for the months in South America, visiting the Baptist churches gave her heart much hope. Some of the little churches were less than weather worthy, but each one she visited was packed to capacity. She loved visiting a little church just beginning in a small adobe home. In contrast was the First Baptist Church of Rio, where her heart thrilled to worship with 1,200 worshippers and participate in the week's evangelistic services led by Dr. Truett. Over 100 professed faith that week.

Nothing thrilled Kathleen more than meeting with WMU societies. Brazil had an incredible 261 societies, and Kathleen stored away the sights and impressions to share with the Union. Along with the many missionary societies, her heart was delighted with the Baptist schools she visited. On the other hand, Kathleen tried valiantly to like Brazilian coffee and could never quite make it, although she smiled graciously as she accepted cup after cup and pretended to drink. And as usual, gift after gift was pressed upon Kathleen — beautiful laces, trays with blue butterfly wings, and exquisite embroidery.

After her eye-opening visit to South American countries, Kathleen corrected her thinking about missionary hardships. For years she had considered that only missionaries to the Orient or those in Africa endured true hardships. Not so. Some South American missionaries labored in places of penetrating cold during the winter, often without even the small comfort of a coal oil stove. And, even harder, some of the missionaries served in terrible loneliness, living and working in isolated outposts. She left with a profound new appreciation for the sacrifice and dedication of hundreds of Baptist missionaries, unsung and unknown, but faithful to their call. Brazil, Peru, Argentina, Panama — on the countries came, and the memories cut permanently into the fabric of her heart. Upon reaching Birmingham early that fall, Kathleen realized she had traveled more than 21,000 miles.

During the trip to South America, just as years before on the trip to the Orient, Kathleen was showered with gifts. A few of the smaller items bestowed by worldwide friends, Kathleen would put in her office. Most gifts, however, had a different use. Occasionally, she gave one to friends or relatives on special occasions, always carefully determining how each would be appreciated. For the most expensive gifts, however, Kathleen had another purpose. These were frequently sold, and the money given to the Lottie Moon or Annie Armstrong offerings. It thrilled her to be able to give more than she normally would have been able to afford.

Kathleen loved to think back to past blessings, like seeing missionaries at work in South America, but she spent the majority of time in putting out fires started every day in the workings of both WMU and the SBC. This was especially the case during the anxiety-fraught years of the Depression. Laura Armstrong's first years as president were extremely difficult as she and Kathleen worked tirelessly together to pull WMU through the Depression. Laura joined Kathleen in championing the efforts of the Hundred Thousand Club, keeping their eyes fixed on the goal of a debtless denomination. By 1934 and 1935, a lot was coalescing in missions advance, and Kathleen and Laura welcomed the help of women who came on board to head up special programs. Olive Martin of Virginia headed up stewardship, and Una led both the personal service and mission study. Sometimes late at night, Kathleen would think back over the myriad activities and projects of the day and recall the struggling little band of women in 1888 who had bravely set out through uncharted waters. Wouldn't they smile to see a veritable fleet of women at work now! Una and Kathleen were jubilant when, at the 1935 annual meeting in Memphis, the two mission boards agreed to a cycle of correlated mission study books.

In September, Kathleen wrote to her friend and co-worker, W.O. Carver at Southern Seminary, rejoicing with the family at the appointment of their cherished daughter Dorothy as a missionary to Japan. In a departure from her usual reticence in sharing her innermost emotions, Kathleen confessed to Dr. Carver that her sentiments were mixed: thrilled for the privilege that was Dorothy's, yet at the same time, sensing a stab of regret in thinking of the long-held desire of her own heart to serve as a missionary in Japan. To add to her joy was the news that Dorothy would be teaching English at Seinan Jo Gakuin. (Several years later, when Dorothy was on furlough, Kathleen and Dorothy roomed together at a conference, and Kathleen drank in stories of God at work in the hearts of students in Fukuoka.)

Kathleen often reflected on lessons learned in these more than twenty years leading Woman's Missionary Union, smiling to think how vehemently she could advocate for an idea or project she felt important. She pondered one day, *I'm a bit like a mother hen guarding her chicks, I guess, with my ideas being those small chicks. And yet, I've learned to wholly support the idea of the majority of these dear women, even if that idea is not the same as mine.* Kathleen gave a gentle sigh, and with a rueful look, admitted that it was not always an easy response. Nonetheless, she was highly gratified at the executive committee's meeting in January, when a chance remark by a convention leader noted this particular tendency she had developed only through years of prayer and learning how to bow gracefully to the inevitable. Stalwart Dr. Ellis Fuller, president of the Home Mission Board, had been present at this meeting. It was a particularly controversial session with much debate. At the conclusion of the session, Fuller was asked to say a word. "Ladies," he declared, "I wish that every preacher in the Southern Baptist Convention could have been here tonight. I didn't know that anybody in the world would ever dare to differ with Miss Mallory. I have heard that she *runs* Woman's Missionary Union. Now I know that she only *helps.*"

During her years as WMU's leader, Kathleen did not fully recognize this ability as one of the underlying strengths of her leadership. She was unbending in her convictions, but equally democratic in her practice. If a motion she fully supported was voted down, she would then unstintingly throw the full weight of her efforts behind the decision of the majority. At the same time, she graciously concealed her own wishes and feelings. This proved the great strength of her remarkable leadership and was one more mark in building the deep respect in which she was held by those with whom she worked.

Even in advance of the 1936 annual meeting in St. Louis, Kathleen and the executive committee were already looking toward the Jubilee to be celebrated in 1938. Likewise, Ethlene Cox was hard at work on the history to be published for that celebration. Meanwhile, Kathleen looked around the vast auditorium in St. Louis and marveled at the sight of more than 2,000 women gathered together to celebrate both a centennial and a special Jubilee, for Sunbeam Bands were recognizing their fiftieth year. Juliette Mather was sparkling with excitement when she introduced their special guest: seventy-six-year-old George Braxton Taylor — "Cousin George," the founder of Sunbeams. The entire body rose to their feet in tribute to this living piece of history in their midst.

Not only a Jubilee but a Centennial as well marked the St. Louis gathering. It was the Shuck Centennial, 100 years of Baptist missions in China. Kathleen and WMU leaders had been planning a year ahead, and the body had designated $30,000 from the 1935 Lottie Moon offering to provide Bible training schools for women in China and to build a school for girls in South China. Kathleen felt personally privileged to be able to speak and memorialize the work of Henrietta Hall Shuck, the beautiful young missionary who had sailed to China as an eighteen-year-old and helped establish schools and churches in that land. Kathleen movingly told of visiting Macau, where Henrietta first began ministry, and then of standing reverently at the grave of Henrietta in Hong Kong. She had died at the age of twenty-seven, leaving forever a legacy in China. Even more emotional to Kathleen was the moment she introduced Mrs. F.Y.O. Ling, president of All-China Woman's Missionary Union, to the body. Speaking in beautiful English, Mrs. Ling paid moving tribute to the life and sacrifice of Henrietta Shuck.

St. Louis had one high moment after another. The great Nannie Helen Burroughs, director of National Baptist Women, was a guest speaker. (She headed the National Baptist Woman's Auxiliary for an incredible sixty-one years.) Nannie was a dynamic speaker, and the women listened raptly to her inspirational message. WMU then presented Nannie Helen a gift to establish a literature department for the national convention. This became an annual gift that supported the literature ministry of National Baptist Women. As Nannie spoke, she brought back special memories for the older women attending the meeting. She recalled how, back in 1901, Annie Armstrong had been her bulwark and support, one of the chief reasons National Baptist Women had organized so effectively. More than thirty years earlier, and serving as Nannie's mentor, Annie helped her design and form a strong women's organization among national Baptists.

This St. Louis meeting marked the beginning of a unique relationship between Nannie Burroughs and Kathleen. Coming from vastly different backgrounds, Kathleen discovered they had so much more in common than either would have believed. The two women were even born in the same year — Kathleen, born to privilege in the heart of the deep South; Nannie born in Virginia, the daughter of a couple who had bought their own freedom in the years before the Civil War. Nannie's mother, Jennie, had been a slave as a child and well remembered when her own parents were allowed to buy their freedom. The desire for independence was bred deep in Nannie's spirit. Kathleen was to glean special blessings and insight both from and through this unique woman, blessings that lasted a lifetime. These same years also brought a new self-understanding to Kathleen that grew in the years that followed.

WMU Jubilee annual meeting, Richmond, Virginia, May 12-15, 1938

CHAPTER NINETEEN

1936-1941

The year 1936 presented some surprising, and quite unexpected, challenges to Kathleen. Union president Laura Armstrong urged Kathleen to represent WMU at the annual meeting of National Baptist Women in Jacksonville in September. Kathleen was most reluctant, insisting to Laura that she was not the best one to speak. Laura persisted, so Kathleen graciously agreed. Immediately, she began preparing and praying for an intuitive caring heart so as to best present a timely message. In her heart of hearts, she recognized that her view of the races was patterned after the accepted standards of her youth. Much of that, in turn, was based on stereotypes. She needed to dig deeper.

Kathleen was warmly received by the National Baptist Women and given attentive ears. She was touched by their loving reception. This was a new experience for her, and she was finding a new balance in her view of race in her own country, having met these brilliant and articulate women who shared the same beliefs and goals that she held. And Kathleen was moved to tears by the beautiful letter of thanks sent to her by Nannie Burroughs, who paid her the high compliment of saying, "Your visit did as much for us as Miss Annie W. Armstrong's visit did in 1900. It set the music of goodwill and Christian cooperation ringing anew in our hearts … The message that came out of your soul struck a responsive chord in their hearts."

As was her custom, Kathleen wrote a confidential report of her work to the executive board of the Union. In it, she used words that caused Una Roberts Lawrence to catch her breath in dismay. Kathleen, in describing the capable women who had led in Jacksonville, referred to one as a "highly gifted mulatto" and another as the "very dusky" leader. And as so frequently happens, the confidential report made its way to a state Baptist paper and was published. Upon learning that the report would be made public, Una contacted Nannie at once and sent her a copy. Nannie, with her capacious heart, immediately responded in redemptive fashion, saying: "This shows how badly we need contact. Poor Miss Mallory doesn't know … . I'm glad you told me. We can help the dear soul, and she will never know it."

Kathleen was a quick learner. This salutary experience was a turning point for her in examining her viewpoint regarding race. When Una diplomatically explained the hurt that could be caused by her choice of terminology, Kathleen was stricken. Never would she knowingly offend anyone. It simply was not in her nature. Kathleen was brutally honest with herself, carefully examining her own heart, struggling to understand that what was simply a way of life — a way of thinking to her — could be condescending and hurtful to others. In the following years, Nannie Helen came to adore Kathleen as they worked in close cooperation and walked some highly unusual paths together. Kathleen struggled to deal with racial prejudice that was an unintentional, but deeply ingrained, part of her life. Bit by bit, she came to understand something of the depth of the thorny problems Burroughs faced every day of her life. The two women became devoted friends and strong partners in ministry.

Often Kathleen would sink into her bed at night — exhausted but grateful for all the ongoing programs and plans for the Jubilee. Plans for a grand celebration were being led by Cora McWilliams of Missouri, who had assigned a veritable army of capable women to work on each aspect of the anniversary that would be held in Richmond — back where it all began in 1888. The 1937 annual meeting in New Orleans in May was built around those preparations just ahead. The evening that the meeting concluded, Kathleen dropped into sleep on the thought that now she had a new title, but she didn't feel one bit different. Well — maybe a bit more tired. WMU had voted that no longer would they have a corresponding secretary but rather an executive director, more in line with the vast responsibilities the office required. A faint smile crossed her face as she decided the title didn't make her one whit wiser. Kathleen was quite oblivious to the fact that most in the convention leadership looked upon her with awe: her stamina, her wisdom, her quiet authority, the weight of her words. Una Roberts Lawrence laughingly told her after one particularly intense meeting that it was a byword in the convention that Kathleen Mallory was "the tiny dynamo."

Sometimes the strain of long hours, much travel, meetings that could seem endless, or new problems coming in quick succession and piling up, overwhelmed Kathleen. She knew in such moments that she needed even more time to pray. A key to her great strength in service was her personal understanding of that utter dependency on the One who had called her. The first day of November 1937, she was far from Alabama on a speaking trip when a telegram arrived. Her oldest brother, Hugh, had died very suddenly. Hugh, the family's rock, especially in the years since her parents' death, was now gone — and gone so young, only sixty-three. Kathleen wept herself to sleep on her knees in prayer, told no one, and finished her schedule on the road. There was no way to get there in time for the funeral, and Hugh was beyond her help now. Nevertheless, the loss of her brother brought anguish to her heart.

Kathleen was amazed to think of the contrast between the little gathering in Richmond in 1888 — when a small but intrepid group of women from twelve states organized the Woman's Missionary Union, Auxiliary to the Southern Baptist Convention — and this year of 1938, with more than 3,500 women regis-tered in Richmond. She thrilled to hear the host of voices singing

"All Hail the Power of Jesus' Name." WMU women from around the world brought stirring messages, and in a parade of states, Kathleen watched as representatives dropped contribution certificates into a golden chest on the platform. She literally felt chills run up and down her spine when the amount was tallied: $60,000 toward the Golden Jubilee goal.

The Jubilee celebration continued from one high moment to another. The auditorium seated 4,656, and an estimated 3,000 people were turned away. In gorgeous color and pageantry, 350 young people presented "The Golden Yesterday, the Golden Today, and the Golden Tomorrow."

The program became personal to Kathleen as she listened to the presentation by Moonbeam Tang, a beautiful young woman from China, who spoke movingly about the atrocities her people were currently suffering at the hands of the Japanese. Seated nearby on the platform at the same time was another program participant, Kiyoko Simose, a bright, young Japanese student. As Moonbeam spoke, Kiyoko sat the entire time with head bowed, eyes downcast. Following Miss Tong's moving words, a period of intercession followed; as all stood with bowed heads, Kathleen quietly stepped to Kiyoko's side and gently placed her arm around the young student.

The entire body was moved when a message from Annie Armstrong was read. Annie was eighty-eight years old and bedridden in Baltimore, but included in her message were the two words forever linked with her great legacy: Go Forward. (Seven months later, Annie Armstrong went forward to her eternal reward.) A year later, the annual meeting was built around the legacy of Annie Armstrong. Kathleen was grateful that the location for the meeting was Oklahoma City. How appropriate it was to be in the state where Annie had lavished her love on the Indians of the various tribes and where she, in turn, had been so loved by them. Kathleen beamed as she sat on the platform observing members of the Fairfax, Oklahoma, missionary society present their program, all of them appearing in costume. Mrs. John Smith, a Creek Indian, told of Miss Annie riding onto their reservation on horseback and helping them organize the first society among the Indians. Smith herself was one of the girls educated by Annie Armstrong those many years ago. She glowed as she told of the Christmas boxes WMU women from across the South sent to the reservation.

This annual meeting was the first since the death of Annie the previous November, and Kathleen felt honored to be able to pay their great leader tribute: "Miss Annie W. Armstrong, fifty years before, did more than any other one person to consummate the organization now known as Woman's Missionary Union ... It is gratefully believed that she laid at Christ's feet a golden sheaf from her long life of sowing and tending in His many fields." The older women present, a few of whom who could remember Miss Annie personally, were especially moved by the quote from Annie herself that Kathleen used to conclude the meeting: "The past is glowing with God's blessings upon the consecrated labors of His children. The future is rich in promise of great things in store."

Just two months later, the Baptist World Alliance (BWA Congress) was held in Atlanta, the city recently taken by storm by the new best seller, "Gone with the Wind." At the Sunday evening service, Kathleen sat near the front of the vast stadium at Ponce De Leon Park and joined some 42,000 Baptists from around the world in singing "All Hail the Power of Jesus' Name." It was unlike any worship experience she had ever known. BWA president George W. Truett was presiding, and WMU's own Ethlene Boone Cox was the evening's featured speaker. Kathleen sat with a little tingle of expectation, for there could be no one in the Union better suited to represent the Baptist women of America than their own Ethlene.

Knowing Ethlene as she did, Kathleen was certain she would be beautifully prepared. Even though she seldom referred to a manuscript, Cox routinely had one prepared. Following a warm introduction by Dr. Truett, tall, elegant, and eloquent Ethlene began her message. The first sentence was scarcely out of her mouth when Kathleen's eyes widened to see a gust of wind sweep across the stadium's platform, taking with it several pages of Ethlene's notes and dropping them at random spots around the stage. Kathleen drew in her breath as she watched the dignified George W. Truett quietly leave his chair, get on his knees, and gather up the errant pages. Even as he completed his task, Ethlene beautifully covered the moment by lifting her hands and said, "Gone with the wind! In what more appropriate place could it have happened than in Atlanta?!" Kathleen heard an appreciative ripple of laughter move through the vast stadium. Ethlene quickly had 42,000 listeners in the palm of her elegant hand.

It occurred to Kathleen that twin realities now confronted WMU, and, indeed, the entire SBC. As women gathered in Baltimore in 1940, two major issues were front and center on most minds: the ever-present specter of debt that had hung over the convention for decades, and, looming even more ominously, the too-real possibility of world war. Denominational debt was not WMU's fault. However, they were determined to attack it head on. Laura Armstrong spoke on "For a Debtless Denomination by 1945" at the Monday morning session. The presidents of both mission boards as well as the seminary presidents brought reports, each explaining what the eradication of debt would mean to their ministry. Several state leaders next walked across the back of the platform, unfurling a huge banner declaring: For a Debtless Denomination by 1945.

That was the cue for Kathleen to go to the podium. She immediately presented the recommendation of the WMU Executive Committee: In light of the Convention's $3 million debt, WMU would pledge to raise $1 million of that amount. The sum was enough to make the delegates swallow hard, but it passed without a question. Charles Maddry, the new president of the Foreign Mission Board, was very moved and spoke emphatically: "We *will* have our debts paid by 1945. WMU has promised, and you can count on them." (Not a day passed in the following five years that Kathleen did not personally make that declaration, for she immediately began using stationery with the letterhead "For a Debtless Denomination by 1945.") Alma Wright, that stalwart champion of stewardship, was named chairman of the drive. Kathleen knew of no one better qualified or equipped than this dear friend. At the close of the session, after Kathleen spoke with great power and emotion, every person present knelt to pray together and pledge themselves to this sacred effort.

For some reason, the past two years had been ones of deep introspection for Kathleen. Possibly, she concluded, it had to do with her age. She had always acknowledged her childlike pleasure in receiving birthday cards. But on the night of January 23, 1939, and one day away from the big 6-0, she wrote her friend Alma Wright, "I feel all of a sudden that a message of commiseration would be more appropriate." Kathleen stood in front of her dresser mirror, looking at herself as she pondered the significance of the milestone. Ever honest with herself, she thought with candid self-reflection, *I am now sixty years old. I must consider — what have I done with my sixty years?* Should any of the thousands who knew Kathleen have answered her heart cry, she would have heard so clearly of the many things she had *indeed* accomplished during those sterling sixty years. However, Kathleen felt as if the specter of old age was staring her in the face. In ten years or less, she must retire. So much to do — so little time in which to do it.

Frugal from habit, Kathleen had not even owned a radio until just a few years earlier, when her nieces and nephews decided to rectify that at Christmas in Selma. Kathleen took a huge delight in listening to beautiful classical music and to hymns late in the evening, often when doing her mending or, more frequently, finishing up editing on yet another edition of *Royal Service*.

Her faithful secretary, Mary Godwin, noticed something a bit unusual about Kathleen those months of 1939. She had always come to the office becomingly dressed but now, Mary noticed, she was actually using a touch of rouge — not that she would have dared voice her observation. Mary later discovered that one of Kathleen's nieces had managed to effect the change. Kathleen's niece had gently encouraged her to use just a touch of rouge. "No, I *do* not want to." "But, Artie, even Susan Anderson — and you know you call her a most heroic missionary — considers it good judgment." "I *do* not want to," Kathleen insisted. At the moment, the two were standing in the wings of an auditorium stage just before the last session of a state convention. "Well, Artie, your face is shiny. May I touch it lightly with a puff?" Kathleen sighed a bit and murmured resignedly, "I guess." And quick as a butterfly's wings, a whiff of pale pink powder was whisked over her cheeks. And, just as reluctantly, Kathleen admitted she rather liked the healthy look. She began using it sparingly but regularly.

A friend of Kathleen's from high school days was now a semi-invalid. One day as Kathleen visited her, the dear woman began weeping, declaring the terrible loneliness of her life. Taking her hands, Kathleen gently reminded her, "I *know* how it feels to be lonely, but I know there is One whose comradeship is yours for the asking."

Increasingly hovering on the horizon was the threat of global war, one of proportions never before imagined. Even as WMU kept meeting the challenges of stewardship, the inevitability of war grew closer. By 1940, the headlines were sounding more ominous by the day. One day, the *Birmingham News* read: "Japan Joins Rome-Berlin Axis"; another day, "Fierce Battle of Britain"; and one morning, "Christian Missionaries Evacuating Asia and Europe." Then came the stark headlines on December 7, 1941: "1,500 Dead in Hawaii: Congress Votes War." World War II had begun.

Portrait of Kathleen Mallory
near retirement

CHAPTER TWENTY

1941-1945

Oh God, sustain us. Oh God, protect Your people. Grant us grace upon grace. Cries to God for help in time of need tumbled around Kathleen's mind. The horrors of war were upon the nation, and Kathleen's heart was wrenched. Prayer alone sustained her, giving her grace and strength to meet the needs of others and fulfill her responsibilities in the face of grave challenge. War was also deeply personal. Four of her beloved nephews were in military service, and all too soon came word that one was grievously wounded. Hugh Mallory Stewart, her sister Irma's second son, came home a paraplegic to spend his life in a wheelchair. (In his beautiful acceptance of his situation, she saw a striking example of courage in the face of adversity.) Kathleen did not know even one family that was untouched by the world conflict. She prayed long and hard for the hundreds of missionaries overseas, so many of them in harm's way. Then there were the believers in these countries, many of them undergoing unimaginable suffering, some of them dying. She was shocked to hear news about Laura Lee Patrick Munger, her dear friend and co-worker those many years ago in Alabama WMU days. Laura Lee and her husband were put in a concentration camp in the Philippines, prisoners of the Japanese. Kathleen woke every morning with Laura Lee on her heart.

Dealing with the fallout from World War II simply made Kathleen's challenging job just that much more formidable. Many mornings she realized that she was feeling so exhausted simply because she did not have enough time to sleep. And, as more and more women entered the workplace out of necessity, Kathleen was gratified to see evening businesswomen's circles multiply. The youth organizations were growing as well, and Kathleen breathed a sigh of gratification when WMU hired Ivyloy Bishop to work with Royal Ambassador (RA) camps. He became the first man employed by WMU for professional work.

A special ministry was developed through funds designated in the Jubilee offering. That, too, presented a lot of new challenges for Kathleen. WMU planned a series of interracial institutes, with the idea of training black women as leaders of missionary societies in their churches. The training had been tried successfully in

Virginia and Oklahoma, so a committee from WMU's ranks
began an extended strategy. Kathleen made the whole plan an
item of intense prayer. She felt it so important an undertaking
that she canceled a number of her usual responsibilities in 1940
and led the coordinating effort for the first of three summers
of interracial institutes. The letters between Nannie Helen and
herself grew in number until they literally exceeded a ream.
Along with the volume of correspondence grew her appreciation for Nannie Helen's courage and the magnitude of problems
that the great lady faced simply in the process of performing her
duties. Life was a major challenge for a black woman in 1940s
America in the South. Kathleen went to great lengths to make
it possible for Nannie Helen and her leaders to even *get* to the
institutes. Kathleen went to personally visit a station master and
make special arrangements for Nannie and her staff to travel on
the trains. Frequently, she also had to contact the management of
a hotel to make special arrangements for Nannie to be allowed
to enter the hotel and come to one of the conference rooms for
a meeting. On one occasion, Kathleen looked back over a letter
she had written about preparations for Nannie to meet with a
committee at a hotel. It had taken six pages of handwritten direc-
tions to make sure her friend had access to that particular hotel in
the heart of the deep South.

For three consecutive summers, highly successful biracial
institutes were held in Mississippi, Alabama, and Georgia. They
were a huge success. Nannie was in a New York City hospital
recovering from cancer surgery the first summer but somehow
managed to advise Kathleen in her plans. Kathleen was in awe

of Nannie's skill and dedication in the face of personal suffering. One of Nannie's fellow leaders was M'bola Ayorinde of Nigeria, a brilliant and dedicated WMU leader from that country. M'bola was shocked at the stumbling blocks put in her way in America simply because of the color of her skin. Kathleen, through all the process of planning and teaching and working with the dedicated women of the National Baptist Convention, came to a new understanding of race in America and gained insight into some of her own personal misconceptions.

She also came to a new appreciation for the largeness of Nannie Helen's soul. Nannie displayed a remarkable tolerance for the misconceptions and deep-rooted prejudices of so many white women. In a letter to her friend Una Roberts Lawrence, Nannie Helen wrote quite poignantly, "I love your race a great deal more than they love me." Due to that leader's generous heart, the mutual respect she and Kathleen shared bridged the gap created by America's cultural history. One of the institutes was held in Kathleen's hometown, Selma, on the campus of Selma University. That was the first of a number of times that Kathleen had opportunity to visit the campus and work with the faculty and students there. One of the most meaningful moments of her years as executive director came when Selma University awarded her an honorary doctorate. Kathleen was asked to address the student body, and her voice rang out clearly in the crowded auditorium as she challenged the graduates. She was then visibly moved when Dr. William Dinkins, the university president, placed the doctoral hood around her neck.

All logistical problems notwithstanding, nearly 900 women

attended the three institutes that first summer of 1940. Kathleen led in planning and conducting the training sessions for four summers. They spread to eight southern cities and reached over 5,500 women. Through those efforts, the work of National Baptist Women grew exponentially as did Kathleen's love and admiration for Nannie Helen Burroughs. At the end of the years of institutes, Kathleen looked back at the masses of correspondence she had exchanged with Nannie, remembered the thousands of logistical hurdles they had overcome, and knew beyond doubt that it was all well worth it.

Even in the face of world conflict, the work of WMU went on. The task was beyond her skills. Kathleen realized that it simply called for even more reliance on God. She never issued an official position on war issues but bravely directed women throughout the Union in alleviating needs and offering practical help. WMU enrollment during the war years declined at the outset, but contributions actually increased. Kathleen and her team in Birmingham had to wage a constant battle to get paper supplies for printing WMU magazines. Kathleen was nothing loath to call on two family friends in the US Congress to intercede in getting paper to print *Royal Service*.

The theme for the 1942 annual meeting in San Antonio was "Expect — Attempt," the two signal words from William Carey's famous quote: "Attempt great things for God; expect great things from God." This was the sesquicentennial of Carey's arrival in India and the genesis of the modern missionary movement. Juliette Mather already had a strong reputation as a "pageant maker" and directed a stirring pageant in San Antonio celebrating Carey's arrival in India. Many women could not get to the gathering because of rationing of gas, but the meeting was particularly uplifting for those who could make it. As conditions continued to tighten, Kathleen consulted her executive committee to consider what to do about the 1943 meeting. The decision was tough, but Kathleen saw no good alternative — so there *was* no annual meeting. Kathleen sent a book of reports to each state and encouraged them to have local or regional gatherings. The following year, the annual meeting was not a typical one either. Because of dire war conditions, no one city could handle both the SBC and WMU at the same time, so, in 1944, WMU met separately in Oklahoma City. The delegates unanimously reelected Laura Armstrong as president, and they were shocked and saddened when she stated that it would be her last year to be able to accept the office. For years, her blood pressure had been growing increasingly elevated and was now quite dangerous.

Kathleen was daily becoming more aware of the inevitable changes that would occur in the nation following the war, and she knew that WMU would need to meet the challenge of another century. Now was the time to begin planning. And, to herself each night as she sank wearily into her bed, Kathleen was all too aware that she could not serve long enough to effect the changes that must come. She was also painfully conscious of the reality of her years. The older she got, the more change hurt. Here it was 1944, and Kathleen realized that a conclusion to the dreadful war must surely come soon. There would need to be cataclysmic changes at WMU to meet a changing world, and she was already sixty-five years old. She couldn't continue much longer at this pace, and her doctor's warnings were ringing in her ears: "Miss Mallory, your blood pressure is getting too high. You *must* work with less stress." Already, she felt the effects of more than thirty years of constant going and doing and leading. Was not Laura Armstrong's health a sober reminder of human frailty, and Laura was considerably younger than she? Change must come.

Two years earlier, Kathleen had first mentioned to Laura the need for a thorough survey of needed changes in WMU, and a clear look at future goals. In February 1944, she asked Laura to select a committee to study how the Union could best carry forward its purpose in promoting missions in the dawning of a new era. Laura appointed Cora McWilliams of Missouri as chair of the survey committee, asking her to bring a report to the January 1945 executive board meeting. Kathleen felt a certain measure of peace in realizing that WMU could, at the very least, attempt to be adequately prepared to embark on its second century.

The committee brought its report in January 1945. They had surveyed pastors, missionaries, state WMU leaders and Woman's Missionary Society members in churches. Some of the findings were disturbing, and some of its recommendations quite startling. Opinions varied so widely that the report actually strained some long-held friendships. Laura appointed several committees to set in motion some of the new ideas. There were many facets to the report, and most of its ideas and suggestions were quietly put into motion by Kathleen herself. Meanwhile, the report in its entirety was so controversial that Kathleen sealed it in a vault; it was to be read only by permission of the president. Kathleen personally continued praying for God's guidance for her in the years following the war. She felt there needed to be new eyes and new ideas focused on bringing in a new era. She was determined to be able to hand off to WMU's next leader a viable and thriving organization, one thriving on serving.

With conditions made difficult by war and rationing, Kathleen's office needed to increasingly depend on volunteers to get needed work done and magazines ready to mail on time. Women young, and not so young, never came away from WMU headquarters without a feeling of accomplishment and a sense of well-being. Miss Mallory always called them "my volunteers," and would so denote them when visitors were in the building. One young volunteer recalled her impressions on WMU's leader, remembering above all else Miss Mallory's dependence on prayer. "Each time I arrived, Miss Mallory would put her hands on my shoulders, look into my eyes and smilingly say, 'We are going to pray before we lift a finger.' And when we volunteers were assembled, she would tell the group, 'We are going to pray about this, to see what we need to do.' Immediately, she would kneel in prayer, right where she was, and all of us would follow suit." The volunteer concluded, "I never left that office without feeling worthwhile. What a special lady!"

War was still raging, and WMU was still working toward a debtless denomination. As usual, each night Kathleen would assess where they stood at debt reduction, never easing up on keeping the need before the faithful women of WMU. Ever on her mind was the debt and WMU's goal. She and other leaders were determined to meet their personal goal of $1 million. Amazingly — and despite war conditions — the amount women gave toward a debtless denomination grew each year. On March 11, 1943, Kathleen called Alma Wright, chairman of WMU's stewardship committee, to tell her a telegram had just come from the Foreign Mission Board. They were debt free! The Home Mission Board took longer, but finally 1944 arrived, and the convention was blessedly free of debt. The burning question for Alma Wright and the women of WMU was: Did we meet our million-dollar quota? March blew in, and still they did not know. Meanwhile, Alma Wright lay in a Birmingham hospital, desperately ill. Every evening after work, for seven straight weeks, Kathleen made her way to the hospital, checking on her dear friend, talking quietly and soothingly, and always ending the evening with prayer. Alma's question each evening as Kathleen entered her room, "Have you heard? Did we meet the quota?" A few days before Alma's death, Kathleen walked into the room and, taking one look at her face, her friend's wan face lighted up. She breathed, "We met it, didn't we?" Kathleen knelt beside the bed, and they joyfully thanked God together. As Kathleen left that night, she paused at the door and looked back to see written across her friend's face a look of ineffable peace. Just days later, with her daughter Annie and Kathleen both at her side, Alma Wright quietly passed into eternity.

Laura would officially complete her duties at the May meeting of the Union, but there was no meeting in 1945 due to war conditions. On Mother's Day 1945, Laura Armstrong, only fifty-nine years old, died of a cerebral hemorrhage. When the telegram arrived with the shattering news, Kathleen wept over the loss of a close friend. The last years had been devastating to Kathleen in terms of losing dear ones. First, she had lost her sister Bessie, and in just the second year of the war, her sister Louise had died. Then she lost her cherished friend Alma Wright, and, as with each loss, she shed her tears in private, mentally girded her loins, and quietly returned to work.

First Baptist Church, Selma, Alabama:
Kathleen Mallory's home church

CHAPTER TWENTY-ONE

1945-1948

Kathleen woke early the morning of May 8, 1945, and turned on the morning news, only to hear the staggering news: Germany Surrenders. In typical Kathleen style, she fell to her knees and thanked God, followed by a fervent petition that Japan would soon follow suit. *God help our nation finally see an end to war.* This stunning news was followed on August 6 with the headline: Atom Bomb Dropped on Japan. Horror mingled with relief — great waves of sorrow over the devastation of Hiroshima in her beloved Japan, yet profound relief that this must signal the end of armed combat. By mid-August, the surrender was official, and the nation could begin to heal.

The end of war marked for Kathleen what she considered as her last years as WMU's leader. She saw as her call the need to leave WMU as strong as she could and pass the baton of leadership to the one God already had in mind. All these thoughts were for the moment locked in her heart. Kathleen resolved to methodically work through details and pass on to her successor a thriving organization, one with a strong vision. However, she believed that for now her decision should remain private.

Presently, women had business to conduct, but no president and no annual meeting at which to elect one. In July, the executive committee met at the Tutwiler Hotel in Birmingham and selected Olive Martin, longtime president of Virginia WMU, as the new president. As editor of *Royal Service,* Kathleen had the pleasure of introducing Olive to all the women of WMU through the magazine's pages, writing, "She is an expert parliamentarian, a most gracious presiding officer, the possessor of a most pleasing voice, a tireless worker for and in the missionary education of WMU young people, withal a lady of exceptionally sweet spirit." Kathleen realized that Olive would be the fifth and last president with whom she would work, but now was not the right time to introduce this thought. Olive needed the opportunity to begin in an established system.

Even as World War II ended, both mission boards celebrated their hundredth anniversaries. WMU was happy to pledge its help in the Centennial Crusade to win a million people for Christ and to raise $20,000,000 for mission outreach. WMU renewed its commitment to be *auxiliary* to the convention in the very best sense of the word. Meanwhile, thousands of boxes of food and supplies were sent by societies and individuals to suffering Baptists both in Europe, China and Japan. Kathleen made her own special little box to fill with her cash offering for world relief. For years, it had been her habit to keep an accurate record of daily expenditures for food. Each night before going to bed, she would put into her love box at least an amount equal to what she had spent for food that day. Strangely, when her diet was especially spartan, the little collection box grew heavier. When she would go to a cafeteria or restaurant for lunch, there would pop into her mind's eye the picture of a starving child or a leprous beggar stretching out his hand for help. Kathleen would take a deep breath and decide that maybe today she would have a nourishing bowl of vegetable soup instead of the chicken special.

In all WMU literature in 1945 and in Kathleen's messages as she spoke, there was a golden thread of emphasis on prayer. The second half of the year, her speaking schedule was especially full. And, when Kathleen was in Birmingham, she was invariably the first to arrive at the office in the morning and one of the last to lock up at the end of the day. One active and observant state president warned a newly elected president from a neighboring state not to be fooled by Kathleen's appearance. "Kathleen's fragile beauty is deceptive," she said on a smile. "For years, she has lived a life calling with the constitution of a circuit rider!"

At the January 1946 executive committee meeting in

Birmingham, word came that the Lottie Moon Christmas Offering had for the first time passed the $1 million mark. Upon hearing the news, Kathleen exclaimed, "Oh, friends, let us pray!" She sank to her knees, and the entire committee followed suit. The president murmured, "Miss Mallory, you lead us," and Kathleen poured out a moving hymn of thanksgiving for this avenue of taking salvation to the world's lost people. Those new on the committee were astounded at the depth of beauty of that simple prayer. Miss Mallory spoke as a child to her father. They had never heard anything like it.

An annual meeting could finally be held again, and Miami was the venue for the 1946 gathering. Since 1942, WMU had only been able to have one regular annual meeting, so Kathleen was as excited as if this were her first. Olive Martin was officially elected by the delegates in Miami and presided with ease — her rich, vibrant voice a pleasure to hear. Olive, having been a WMU president since the tender age of twenty-two, appeared perfectly at ease at the podium. Kathleen looked out over the large crowd, and her eyes glowed with thankfulness for being able to experience once again the deep satisfaction of meeting as a body. Small and slender in frame she might be, but Kathleen Malory was undoubtedly the most quietly powerful woman in the Southern Baptist Convention. The meeting's speakers this year were a personal thrill to her, for not only were the heads of both mission boards present and participating, so also was Dr. Rushbrooke, president of the BWA, as well as two of America's most famous pastors — Miami's own C. Roy Angell and R.G. Lee of Memphis. Both pastors were masters of storytelling. R.G. Lee thoroughly enjoyed reminiscing about his early years as a Sunbeam.

Although the aftermath of war brought many changes, one thing did *not* alter: the constant efforts of convention leaders to count WMU's two offerings as part of the overall percentage of funds going to the two mission boards. And WMU, just as consistently and kindly as ever, continued to adamantly oppose such a plan. Some of the more seasoned leaders began to feel like a broken record, but they were convinced of the need to hold their ground.

W.O. Carver was a special blessing to Kathleen in the final years of her leadership. He was WMU week's Bible study leader at Ridgecrest, and thousands of women were spiritually enriched thereby. So many wanted to hear Dr. Carver that the studies were held in Spilman, the largest auditorium. Before the first week ended, women were clamoring for him to return in the same role the next summer, and he graciously agreed. Carver also wrote Bible studies for *Royal Service,* and thousands of women saved their copies each month for further study. In one article, Carver wrote: "The women of 1888 showed a 'holy courage' in their organizing for the support of the missionary work of the boards of the SBC." Carver felt that WMU having organized as an auxiliary was divinely inspired and one secret of their great success. Kathleen wrote to Dr. Carver in July 1945, thanking him yet again for championing WMU throughout the entire convention: "I feel the vast majority of Southern Baptist pastors look to you for guidance in denominational affairs. Therefore, I am as honest as I know how to be in saying that I feel you have made another real contribution to the present and future of our Union by your writing."

In the fall of 1946, Kathleen took on a task that she knew was far too strenuous, yet she felt this would be her last opportunity with the women of Alabama. It was an invitation she did not want to refuse. Alabama WMU had ten district meetings, entailing 2,000 miles of travel plus speaking in one place one day, another town the following, and some of them all-day sessions and still others with young people's meetings that same night. It was a benediction for her heart — the joy of time with the women she had cut her missions teeth on, she thought with a little smile on her face. Those women, some who had been young when Miss Mallory first spoke in their districts in 1910, remembered the lovely young state secretary who had now beautifully fulfilled a lifetime of faithful witness.

Many of the women traveling to the 1947 annual WMU meeting were thinking of the song they had learned as young girls, "Meet Me in St. Louis," and anticipating another high time of inspiration. Kathleen traveled by train from Birmingham, her thoughts keeping pace with the rapidly turning wheels. She knew the months to follow were going to be some of the most difficult of her life, although she had prayed long and earnestly over the issue of retirement. Prior to the opening session, she found a private moment with Olive Martin, telling her of the decision that this would be her last year as director. Looking earnestly into Olive's eyes and placing a gentle hand on her arm, Kathleen spoke as matter-of-factly as she could: "You see, by resigning during the sixtieth anniversary of Woman's Missionary Union, I can pass on to my successor the high privilege of leading the Union into another era." Her voice broke briefly as she added, "And I shall pray God she may excel as no other has yet done." Olive agreed that this would not be made public until January of the next year. In the ensuing months Kathleen discovered how incredibly difficult this was, and so many times, came close to revealing her plans. But, it was her deep conviction that a whole year of thinking about impending change would be harmful to WMU and its work.

St. Louis had a sparkle all its own, for two fortieth anniversaries were to be celebrated. Both the Woman's Training School and Young Woman's Auxiliary had reached that new milestone. Several hundred YWA members were seated on a raised platform, forming the shape of a living YWA emblem in black against a background of white. The effect was stunning. A number of leaders — including Alma Hunt, dean of women at William Jewell College — spoke of the contributions of YWA to their lives. On the heels of this session, the meeting of the executive committee that followed brought a proposal in keeping with the findings of the survey committee. Delegates voted to purchase property in Birmingham to build a headquarters building. In addition, the committee voted to set into motion plans for establishing an editorial department. Kathleen sat quietly, nodding in agreement with the decisions being made. This simply affirmed to her heart that she was indeed making the decision God would have her make. Now, with so many needed changes in the offing, was the proper time to let changes begin with fresh new leadership. Right on the heels of the thought, her heart felt a stab of pain as she recognized the personal agony the change would mean for her. She later confessed the depth of her heartache to her sister, "Irma,

I can only express it this way. I love the Union better than my life,"
and the pain in her voice was almost tangible.

Keeping her plans to herself was a steady exercise in discipline
for Kathleen — but then, a lifetime of personal discipline was
standing her in good stead. Mary Godwin, her private secretary
for a dozen years, had no idea, for Miss Mallory conducted her
daily work with her usual gracious, efficient thoroughness. Mary
somehow never thought of Miss Mallory except as a lovely,
cultured single lady, wholly dedicated to Woman's Missionary
Union. However, one morning in September, Mary had a surprise.
An elderly, unmarried visitor had been in the office with them
for some time chatting, and somehow the conversation turned to
the limited number of career opportunities open to women when
the century had begun. The visitor commented, "For those of us
who did not find a husband, only school teaching was possible."
About that time, someone came to the door and summoned the
visitor to go with them to a conference. Mary was startled when
Miss Mallory looked her way with a mischievous twinkle in her
eyes, raised her eyebrows and exclaimed "*Pshaw! Any* woman can
get married. Why, Mrs. Godwin, I had plenty of beaux — just
plenty of them!" The unexpected openness on Kathleen's part set
Mary Godwin to looking at her boss with new eyes. She suddenly
imagined Miss Mallory's desk as a table, set with a cloth of Brussels
lace. Her finely shaped hands weren't holding a pen and paper, but
instead, a dainty silver teapot and a china cup. Her gown was still
blue (Mary couldn't imagine changing the color), but the fabric
was velvet. The lovely face with its crown of wavy hair looked the
same. Yes, she might have been mistress of a gracious southern

home. There were depths to this amazing leader of women that Mary had never before considered.

Kathleen felt the burden of her impending retirement becoming increasingly heavy and determined that the time was near for her to set plans into motion. On Friday night, January 30, following the last session of the January executive board meeting, Kathleen drew a tired breath, rolled a sheet of paper into her typewriter and started her letter of resignation. Naming the various new plans and new positions and personnel voted into place, and calling attention to plans for a new headquarters building, she wrote that it was her conviction that new staff needed to begin their service:

> ... under the advice of the executive secretary who will have the management of the long anticipated building. I am now sending my resignation to our president with whom I have frankly conferred ... It is highly gratifying to me that our president agrees with me that it is most logical that a new WMU executive secretary be elected at our annual meeting in May ... Because I am certain that the work of these three secretaries should develop side by side as the years come and go, and because I love the Union better than I love my own life, I find it easier than otherwise it could possibly be to ask the WMU Nominating Committee to refrain from submitting my name for re-election in May.

That night, Kathleen slept more soundly than she had in months. Carrying around the burden of her impending resignation had felt like a cumbersome weight. At least she could now face each day with the knowledge that she was fulfilling her mission in an orderly fashion. Her days were full of preparations for the sixtieth anniversary coming in Memphis in May, and at which she would step down as executive director. Sarah Hurst Burney, longtime WMU leader and head of the Margaret Fund scholarship committee, was named chair of the sixtieth anniversary committee. Sarah issued a request to all WMU members to reread *In Royal Service* and *Following in His Train,* the two history books about WMU's first fifty years. Sitting in the little armless rocker in her apartment on quiet Sunday afternoons, Kathleen joined women across the Union in refreshing her memory of years gone by as she read the two volumes again.

As soon as Kathleen had written her letter to the executive committee, she wrote to her dear friend Alma Wright's daughter, Annie, explaining: "One of the hardest things I have ever had to do was to wait until the decision would be made public before telling it to you … I have cried often over my decision. However, I believe it was right … . I have a quiet peace in my heart now that the decision has been made public."

In the spring, Kathleen attended her own Alabama state meeting and was nearly overwhelmed to learn that the state mission offering was to be named in her honor. And, typical for Kathleen, her main gratification about the honor was that it meant the surname of her father would thus be perpetuated among Baptists in Alabama. As the time for her final annual meeting as director grew closer, her tension grew along with it, mainly because she feared breaking down when she stood to speak words of farewell. "I am afraid," she told her sister Irma, "that my tears will make the Mississippi overflow again!" Over and over, she begged Olive Martin to let her be excused from the Memphis meeting. The president was consistently kind and just as consistently firm. Each time her response was the same: "It is your duty to go." And always, Olive would gently add, "You will enjoy it, Miss Mallory."

May arrived, and Kathleen nervously boarded the train for Memphis. Sarah Burney was going to room with her, and the two friends traveled together. Quite unexpectedly, a lovely surprise awaited "the tiny dynamo" in Memphis.

Kathleen Mallory at dedication of Baltimore Mallory Center, 1951

Chapter Twenty-Two

1948-1952

*K*athleen and Sarah Burney checked into their Memphis hotel and quickly headed to their room to unpack and prepare for the first session. Sarah walked over to the window and pretended to be looking at the Memphis street scene far below. Never one to waste time, Kathleen took off her hat, unlocked her suitcase, and took out her neatly folded dresses. They needed to be hung up immediately. She proceeded to open the closet door, and to her shock, her namesake niece was standing inside. "Artie!" exclaimed Kathleen, and "Kathleen!" echoed her aunt, and they hugged each other fiercely. Kathleen turned quickly to see Sarah Burney standing with a satisfied smile on her face. "You knew this!" Kathleen exclaimed. "Indeed, I did," her friend rejoiced, "and I'm going to a room just down the hall. And, by the way," she paused significantly, "there is *another* beloved one on this floor who is eagerly waiting to see you. You needn't be in suspense, though," Sarah smiled. "It's Laura Lee Patrick Munger!"

Those two "beloveds" had been especially invited by Olive Martin as special guests of Woman's Missionary Union. Kathleen's joy was so unexpected, so real, that she scarcely knew whether to cry or to laugh. Laura Lee's torture and incarceration in the Japanese prison camp in the Philippines took its toll on her body, but strengthened her wonderful spirit. For Kathleen, the presence of two so dear to her own heart made the angst of experiencing farewells in such a public setting much less severe than she had anticipated. Hundreds of women found opportunity during the sixtieth anniversary to express their love and appreciation personally to their beloved Miss Mallory. The pageant at this meeting was the most magnificent yet, as it depicted the sixty years of WMU, concluding with the climactic episode that presented Kathleen Mallory as the "queenliest of them all," having served the Union from 1912 to 1948. Laura Lee Patrick Munger had prepared a beautiful tribute, speaking of "The King's daughter … all glorious with — her clothing of wrought gold." And WMU chose to convert that gold into gifts in Kathleen's honor: $100,000 toward a new headquarters building in Birmingham and $100,000 from the Lottie Moon Christmas Offering for building Mallory Hall, the chapel building on the campus of Seinan Jo Gakuin, the school in Japan so special to Kathleen's heart. There was one more allocation: $100,000 from the Annie Armstrong Offering for a new goodwill center in Baltimore, where Kathleen first took up the leadership of WMU in 1912.

The emotional strain of the entire meeting was monumental for Kathleen. She had long been praying that she would manage to have grace for each moment, and she did not break down. Each time she spoke throughout the days, not just she, but those who heard her, sensed a higher power in control of her heart and her words. Rather than giving her printed report as the annual message, she asked that the delegates simply accept the report as printed. She then proceeded to speak from her heart, expressing deep gratitude for all who were her co-laborers. At the conclusion, Kathleen opened the Bible Grandmother Moore had given her in 1912. She had used it at her inauguration in 1912, at the 1913 Jubilate, and the 1938 Jubilee. And now for the last time, she once again raised her melodic, rich voice to read Revelation 5:6-14, ringing with its thrilling message: "Worthy is the Lamb."

The program included numbers of missionaries who, at various sessions, were presented in three groups by their area of the world. With each group, Kathleen would stand in their midst and to the new appointees in each group, she spoke:

The Lord bless thee and keep thee,
The Lord make His face to shine upon thee,
And be gracious unto thee:
The Lord lift up His countenance upon thee,
And give thee peace.

At the close of the pageant, a great replica of the WMU pin was spotlighted — the Word, the world, the burning torch, and the motto "Laborers together with God." The women forever remembered that tableau and the memories of Kathleen Mallory, whose words and presence were as a benediction for that high hour.

In the following years, Kathleen could look back with joy at the beauty of so many high moments in Memphis and rejoice again that she could share it with her namesake. Earlier in the year, when receiving her resignation letter, the executive board had tasked the nominating committee with the responsibility for searching out the one God would have as Kathleen Mallory's successor. Committee chair Cora McWilliams of Missouri traveled to Liberty, Missouri, to approach Alma Hunt, the dean of women at William Jewell College. Hunt, an alumna of Sunbeams, GAs and YWA, was an administrator and compelling leader, but her immediate response upon being told she was the committee's choice was to exclaim in shock, "But I'm not a speaker." In later years, the captivating and remarkable speaker, Alma Hunt, was reminded of those early words she had spoken. Kathleen had the deep satisfaction of being present when Alma Hunt was elected as her successor, secure in the knowledge that her beloved Union was in good hands.

Alma Hunt needed to finish several commitments to William Jewell College and was not able to take up her new position until September. Kathleen agreed to remain until that time and wrap up her many areas of responsibilities, one of the largest of which was the editorship of *Royal Service*. The magazine was now taking the missionary message into 181,000 homes each month. Kathleen felt like she was turning over a cherished child into the hands of others. Letters began to fly back and forth with Alma Hunt, as Kathleen shared information and ideas. During that four-month interim period, she was gradually relinquishing responsibilities into new hands. Hunt also asked Kathleen to spend two weeks at headquarters after her own arrival in Birmingham to help expedite the change of leadership.

Just two days before that final week ended, however, Kathleen confessed to herself that she could not face the final goodbyes. At home in her little apartment, she wrote a personal note of gratitude and love to each person with whom she worked. On her final day in the office, she took the notes with her and, a few hours later, while having lunch with Alma Hunt, told her, "If you don't mind, I am not coming back. I have left a sheaf of notes on the desk. You will distribute them, won't you?" she looked earnestly into Alma's face. Glimpsing just a bit of the quiet pain in Kathleen's eyes, Alma gently responded, "You know I will be so glad to," and reached out to grasp her hand.

The next day, Alma discovered that one of the notes was addressed to her personally, a note in which Kathleen expressed her deep gratitude for Alma's beautiful spirit and declaring, "I want to be faithful in praying for you and all who will be associated with you in the work there and throughout the Union." That last night, Kathleen quietly waited until everyone had left the building. She then gathered up the few remaining items on what had been her desk, stopped at the door to look back at the room one more time, and with her heart feeling both heavy yet paradoxically light at the same time, locked the door of the building and headed home.

It had been one of the longest days of her life.

Kathleen had no intention of being a lady of leisure. It wasn't in her nature. Nor did she intend to be constantly at WMU functions where her successor would be presiding and speaking, for she wanted Alma Hunt to have breathing room to establish her own identity. She did attend all sorts of WMU meetings and traveled to a number of states, but spent much of her time involved in satisfying activities in her home church in Birmingham. In November, Kathleen attended the annual meeting of Alabama WMU and brought the keynote address honoring WMU's sixtieth commemoration year. Immediately upon conclusion of her speech, a motion was made to name the state missions offering for Kathleen Mallory. She was struck speechless by the unexpected honor, and her eyes glistened with tears.

Kathleen discovered she was never bored, for there were always interesting things going on in Birmingham. She was finally able to spend more time serving through her own church, beginning by accepting the responsibility of teaching a large class of women. They were called the JOY class, and they were a weekly joy to their teacher. Most of the group were young matrons, and they fell in love with their lovely and gracious white-haired teacher with the twinkling blue eyes. The class became her "girls," and she grew deeply involved in their joys and sorrows. Each one of them adored her. Kathleen was active in every aspect of church life, and her fellow members soon realized that if there was a service going on, or a project needing help, Miss Mallory was there.

One thing she was determined *not* to do was interfere with Alma Hunt's work, and she resolved early on never again to enter

WMU headquarters. Invitations to come to this or that meeting at headquarters were constantly arriving, but Kathleen graciously and firmly refused. She and national staff, and she and Alma Hunt, frequently met outside the building for lunch or some celebration for a friend, but Kathleen adamantly refused to return to headquarters.

The morning of her birthday in January 1952, the doorbell rang, and she opened the door to see a telegram from Alma Hunt, saying, "May today be the beginning of one of the happiest years of your life. Lovingly, Alma." That same spring, instead of building a new headquarters as had been the plan, WMU was able to purchase an excellent building at a very reasonable purchase price. And, of course, Alma Hunt and all of WMU leadership wanted Kathleen Mallory at the dedication. After all, much of the cost of the building was met by the special gift of WMU women to honor their dear Kathleen Mallory. Still, Kathleen refused. It took the national president, Olive Martin, using pressure tactics to get her to change her mind. Olive Martin convinced her that if she *didn't* come, her absence would be misunderstood; it would be a reflection on herself as president, and especially on the new executive director. That did the trick, for Kathleen's first loyalty was to WMU. The morning of January 21, 1952, Kathleen was present for the dedication and led the dedicatory prayer. She did not know that it was being recorded. In subsequent years, hundreds of Baptists were able to hear the rich and measured tones of Kathleen Mallory's voice, praying as she always did, in a confiding and direct way, as a child to her father.

The following year, seventy-two-year-old Kathleen attended

the dedication of the Mallory Center in Baltimore, named in her honor. Alma Hunt was present for the opening, as were other Baptist leaders. Kathleen spoke to the crowd that had gathered, expressing the hope that, amid tensions all around, the Center might radiate peace and goodwill through lives brought into the kingdom. The Baltimore trip was a nostalgic time for Kathleen. While there, she saw several friends from long-ago college years and reminisced as she visited the school's campus, her church, and other places so cherished in her heart. No memory was more poignant, however, than those of the halcyon days spent in that city with her beloved Janney. The sweet echo of his memory was ever in a treasured corner of her heart.

Nonetheless, Kathleen discovered that the "autumn of life," for all its mellow joys, is never entirely happy. One windy fall afternoon, she paused in the middle of a letter she was writing to glance out at the cloudy day with trees nearly bare of the last leaves, and resumed her letter by writing, "I am a last leaf, like the one on the tree outside my window. All of my immediate family have gone." Just this past year, her sister Irma, the last of her three sisters, had died, and she had also lost her only remaining brother, James. Kathleen had moved into a smaller apartment on Highland Avenue. She could have a refrigerator, but no cooking was allowed. Upon learning this, her nieces and nephews immediately sent a refrigerator. "Artie" thanked them graciously, saying now she could do two cold meals a day at home and eat out the other meal.

She soon discovered, however, that some days she didn't feel well enough to go out. That old nemesis, loneliness, began to rear its spectral head. Prayer had always been a major part of her life, as normal as breathing for Kathleen, and now it became an even greater part of every day. She so literally had the world in her heart that it took hours in prayer to go from continent to continent, lifting missionaries and needs to God in petition. For the young women in her Sunday School class at First Baptist, one of the highlights of each week was when their Miss Mallory led in prayer. That in itself was a worship experience.

During the retirement years, Kathleen had found time to make frequent trips to Selma to be with her many nieces and nephews. She was on one particular trip to Selma and visiting with her niece Jacqueline (Kirby) when she became ill. She was taken to Selma Baptist Hospital, where doctors ran tests to determine her problems. Kathleen dictated a letter to be sent to her Sunday School, a few special friends, and the WMU executive committee, saying, "I have no idea yet when I can get back to Birmingham. When I tell you that I have six family homes here in Selma, you will know that I am surrounded by not only love but real efficient prayer."

The time had been forcibly brought upon her when she would have to make a definitive choice. Many years earlier, Kathleen had intended to retire in Selma, but when retirement time arrived, she had very little immediate family left and had postponed making a decision as to where to live. Now, it seemed the choice was out of her hands. As was her lifelong habit when decisions large and small confronted her, she would immediately pray. That is exactly what Kathleen now did. The answer came. She was ill, she felt the need to be near family, and, therefore, she would move back to Selma.

Kathleen Mallory at dedication of new WMU headquarters, 1952

CHAPTER TWENTY-THREE

1952-1954

There were six homes in Selma that invited Artie to be part of their families, including all her nieces and nephews. Kathleen was most grateful but also extremely realistic. After forty years on her own, she would not be able to easily adjust to being part of a busy family. She graciously responded to each invitation with a "thank you, but I think not." The doctors had warned her that she was going to need to be very judicious with her time and health. Kathleen was facing a fight with anemia, high blood pressure, and heart trouble. It was clearly the breakdown of a worn-out body — not misused, but certainly over-used. When she was able to go back to Jacqueline's home, all the nieces and nephews banded together to persuade their Artie to let them take care of closing out her Birmingham apartment and getting her settled in her own place in Selma. Kathleen was feeling tired enough to know this was a wise move. Jacqueline was a mainstay and looked to her Artie's every need.

Meanwhile, her nephew Edgar, a lawyer and her dear Irma's son, found her a small apartment ideally located right across the street from her own First Baptist Church. To her friends, she wrote: "I know I must not live with any of my nieces or even a certain dear friend here, chiefly because for the past forty-three years I have lived a very independent life and am very opinionated, to put it mildly. The nieces are helping me to get everything in its place. I cannot be thankful enough for their loving and capable service. The apartment is of stucco, two-storied, with ten units. Mine is on the northeast corner of the second floor. From my east windows, I can (and do) look straight across to the beloved First Baptist Church — and on further east to our dear home!"

There were days when she felt quite strong and able to get out and about and follow her own enjoyable routine. On the first Sunday that she felt well enough to attend, she submitted her letter to transfer membership back to First Baptist Church. That February morning brought back such a flood of memories: of the little ten-year-old girl who had dressed in her best blue dress and bonnet, and gathered a little posy of violets to take to church that morning when she publicly professed her faith in Christ. And back came more memories — those of her so-loved pastor, Dr. Frost, and how he had carried little ten-year-old Kathleen into the baptismal waters. This particular morning, sixty-three years later, she nostalgically wore fresh violets, smiling inwardly at her own sentimentality.

First Baptist Selma's missionary society now had a most august addition: their own Kathleen Mallory. To no one's surprise, she quickly became an active member, attending circle meetings and program meetings, and serving as advisor to the Business Women's Circle. Those ladies recognized that a true professional executive was now one of their number. Most of Kathleen's time was spent with family members and with church activities, although she was invited to join a literary club and enjoyed the mental stimulation. The club asked Kathleen to review the new translation of the Bible, the Revised Standard. She was already reading it through from Genesis to Revelation, enjoying new insights. One day a visitor saw the new edition lying in her lap and spoke indignantly, "How can you read that thing? They've even changed our sacred Union motto!"

Kathleen's response was typically calm. "My dear, the basic idea is still inherent in the passage. The beautiful words as we know them will never disappear. They are so indelibly branded in the hearts of Southern Baptist women that we shall always be 'laborers together with God.'" Her visitor was not to be mollified, "And in John 14 they've even taken away our mansions in the skies!" Kathleen replied, a bit of a smile evident in her voice, "For that verse I *prefer* the new translation. You see, if the words are inter-preted literally, far better than a separate mansion is a *room* in the Father's house!" The woman was truly shocked: "You mean you like the new Bible?" "That is my conclusion," Kathleen responded. "The beauty of the King James can never be surpassed, but the new has clarified many obscure passages. We should study both!"

Receiving and writing letters took up much of Kathleen's spare time. She kept the postman far busier than did any other citizen of Selma. Every morning, she received a stack of mail and reveled in the pleasure of hearing from friends and dear ones literally around the world. And there were constant visitors — friends from far away who made occasional pilgrimages, and a steady number who came from WMU headquarters for a brief visit with their beloved Miss Mallory. The nieces and nephews were constantly inviting Artie to come share a meal with them. They all knew that she tended to not take care of herself by spending time preparing nourishing food, so they took care to see that she ate well. The great nieces and nephews in her family always looked upon a visit from the legendary Artie as a special occasion. Edgar's daughter, young Martha Stewart, always understood that when her adored Artie came for dinner, she and her siblings knew to be on their very best behavior. She also knew that dear Artie would be wearing a linen dress in some shade of blue and was certain to have a dainty little white handkerchief tucked in her pocket. And Artie always had such a wonderful store of tales and stories to share, adventures from around the world.

There were several friends from bygone years still living in Selma, and Kathleen loved reminiscing with them on days when she was feeling a bit stronger. She had a marvelous visit with Nellie, her adored nurse of those early years. Nellie was a wonder, well into her nineties and her mind still razor sharp. She and Kathleen chuckled together over some of her childhood pranks. Nellie recounted scattered bits of mischief the Mallory children could come up with, and Kathleen's heart was warmed by precious memories.

Her nephew, Edgar, kept a close and loving eye on Artie and her needs. A prominent lawyer in Selma, he was ever attentive and protective of his beloved aunt. She was the last of that generation remaining and doubly cherished by each niece and nephew. Edgar had a good time teasing her, often reminding her of the "good old days." One afternoon he said, "Artie, can you remember weaning me — on ice cold milk?" "Why, Edgar ..." Kathleen started to protest. "Artie, you know it's the truth. Mother was in the hospital, and I was nine months old and left without food." Kathleen grinned, "And you screamed and refused a bottle." "And you, my intelligent aunt," Edgar picked up the story, "went to the refrigerator, poured some ice cold milk in a tin cup and gave it to the baby." "And you stopped crying!" Kathleen protested. Edgar concluded the tale, "They tell me that from then on I would take nothing except ice cold milk in a tin cup!"

But Edgar wasn't through: "That's not as bad as something else, for which, Artie, I have never forgiven you." Artie grinned, "What did I do?" Edgar told the tale, "It was during those two weeks of the summer when I was nine years old and had committed to your special care while the folks were away." "Yes?" Kathleen sounded interested. "Artie, you made me wash my feet *every* day and ..." "Edgar, you were a dirty little boy." "Yes, but you made me wash my feet every time *before* I got in the tub." And, as Edgar kissed her cheek on a grin and headed back to his law office, Kathleen was smiling and thinking of Edgar, that little boy who, in her eyes, was still the little fellow that she loved so dearly.

Each relative held a special place in Kathleen's heart, and any sorrow or burden they had, she shared with them and prayed God's special guidance for them. But she recognized her own frailty. She just did not talk about it. Shortly before Christmas in 1953, she wrote to Annie Wright Ussery, "I realize that my strength is going rapidly. This I have not said to the dear ones here because I do not like to discuss my illness. It is necessary for me to rest a great deal of the time."

Kathleen was never one to sit around and mope. On the contrary, she loved to dwell on fragrant recollections. Out from under the many years of heavy responsibility, she had come to realize she did not need to fret about wasting time. She did enjoy spending time in beautiful reminiscences and had learned how not to dwell on some long-ago pain or heartache. She would gently allow those to fade away. Sometimes she recalled childhood days, and, in her mind's eye, her brothers and sisters looked as they had as little children. She had outlived all of them. Other times, some fond memory from Christmas with all of them together in Selma would enter her mind and bring a smile to her lips. Even more frequently in her mind's eye were Mother and Father and special moments with one or the other, or both of them. Sometimes she saw them as she remembered them from her childhood days. Then it might be as she last remembered them. There was one face in all her treasured memories, however, that never changed. Janney was forever young and handsome and sweetly smiling in her heart's memory. Those recollections were like a warm blanket that wrapped her in comfort.

During her last few months early in 1954, Kathleen spent much of her time in the hospital. She first suffered a stroke in December and did not have reserves of strength on which to call. Kathleen frequently thought of the old hymn, "Lead me gently home, Father," and rather wryly thought that her home-going didn't feel very gentle. But, then, this was not something that she herself could organize and implement. Surely this was in God's hands. Often, as she reflected on happy memories of her long years of service, she felt a deep gratitude in recognizing that God's design for her life had defined her destiny. What a blessed and comforting thought. Prayer had ever been a major component of Kathleen's life, and now it was even more so. For as long as she could remember, Kathleen's favorite posture for talking with her Heavenly Father was kneeling. Now the time had come when she could no longer kneel and get back up without wrenching pain. As she prayed from her rocking chair, she often reminded her Heavenly Father: *Dear Lord, You know my heart is kneeling before You.*

Then, Kathleen suffered a heart attack and was put in an oxygen tent. Kathleen, Jacqueline, Edgar, and the other nieces and nephews were frequently at the hospital, but they were very careful just to make short, quiet visits and nearly always to bring a beautiful posy of flowers. When the roses began to bloom, Kathleen's eyes would light with pleasure as one niece or the other brought in a beautiful bud or a vase with an eye-catching arrangement. In May, she received a letter from her dear friend Juliette Mather in the Birmingham office. Juliette gently passed on the news that their beloved old man of missions, Dr. W.O. Carver, had entered glory. Kathleen's eyes glistened with tears and she heaved a gentle sigh, knowing with certainty that she would soon be seeing him there.

Kathleen never failed to be grateful to her doctor and the kind nurses who adored and pampered her, and to all the nieces and nephews who showered daily kindnesses on her. Nonetheless, she freely admitted, she was none too happy with hospital discipline. She preferred to walk up and down the hall so that she could prove to her doctor, or sometimes one of her loving relatives, that she was *not* hopelessly ill. She could still get around. The nieces and nephews began to see how frail their Artie was becoming. Sometimes the pain was so intense that her beautiful blue eyes no longer sparkled, but never did her face lose its soft and enduring beauty. There were more and more days when the pain was overwhelming, and still another stroke. And, yet, the perfect peace that came from her closeness to the Heavenly Father gave strength to endure the pain.

Alabama's day of prayer for state missions in 1954 fell on June 17. It never failed to move Kathleen to think that the dear women of Alabama had named the offering in her honor. She had carefully made her offering through the Selma WMU some weeks earlier. During the early hours that morning, Kathleen's breathing began to slow. Then, quite imperceptibly, there came to her face a look of ineffable peace. It could have been that, in those moments, there came softly to her mind's eye the glorified faces of her mother and her father. And, there — ever young, ever smiling — the beloved face of her Janney. But more than any of those, there was the beckoning face of the Savior she had served so long and faithfully, and the voice — *Well done, thou good and faithful servant* — and the outstretched hand.

Stained glass window, First Baptist
Church, Selma, Alabama

EPILOGUE

A rtie had left her treasured nieces and nephews gentle but strict instructions that her funeral was to be short and simple. She requested that Dr. J.T. Pearson, her Selma minister, and Dr. J.T. Ford, her Birmingham pastor, conduct the service. The observance was held in the church where she had been baptized as a little ten-year-old. Now it was her final service there. Selma's historic First Baptist Church featured a number of strikingly beautiful stained-glass windows, including two designed by Tiffany. Kathleen asked her family that there be no expansive eulogy, and her loving nieces and nephews honored her request.

Dr. Pearson, pastor and longtime friend, spoke from his heart, not praising all the significant ways in which she had brilliantly led WMU but instead paying her the highest tribute as he declared, "I think Miss Mallory was the most completely devoted person to Jesus Christ that I have ever known." A beautiful blanket of pink carnations covered the gray casket, and soft organ music played. One close personal friend described the scene as she recalled it: "The late afternoon sun illumined a stained-glass window behind the pulpit and set aglow a white-robed figure of the Christ with hand pointing upward. It seems singularly appropriate to me, that backdrop for our Miss Mallory."

The year following her death, at both the WMU annual meeting in Miami and that of the Southern Baptist Convention, tributes to Kathleen Mallory highlighted each meeting. Her special friend Sarah (Mrs. Frank) Burney conducted the memorial hour for WMU. It was an emotional time for Sarah, who had worked with Kathleen for so many years and had loved and admired her unstintingly. Burney tried to sum up the impact of Kathleen Mallory: "The record of the work of her hands, the triumphs of Christ, are recorded in the history of the Union. Eternity alone will reveal her full attainments for God. She graced — with dignity, consecration, devotion, self-denial, sacrifice and love — the procession of Baptist women whom she led to minister to Jesus." Burney followed with deep-felt tributes from a number of leading Baptist women. Minnie James, longtime national president, said of Kathleen: "With all her winsome, gifted, dynamic personality, her one aim in life was to *know* and *do* the will of her dear Lord." Ethlene Boone Cox, whose friendship and years of working with

Kathleen spanned more than two decades, declared: "Her complete dedication to God in her task and her untiring zeal inspired all who served with her. Her life is not only an important keystone in the structure of Woman's Missionary Union, but is also a capstone ornamenting the enterprise of Baptist world missions."

Ethel Winfield, her former assistant and treasured friend, noted that at the center of Mallory's extraordinary life "was her singleness of purpose. We recall such natural endowments as her winsome presence, her compassionate heart, her mind quick in imagination as well as in analysis and logic, her voice of moving cadence, and her sense of unfaltering honesty." The hundreds of women gathered in the auditorium heard tribute heaped upon accolade, and tears of hallowed remembrance were common in that great gathering.

Before the entire Southern Baptist Convention in general session, high tribute was laid at Kathleen Mallory's feet by women representing both WMU and on behalf of all Southern Baptists. Prominent pastor Dr. John l. Slaughter, who had been Kathleen's minister for many years in Birmingham, honored her memory. Slaughter touched on every aspect of her remarkable leadership, commenting on the unusual blending of the many Christian graces. He called her "a royal soul with the common touch, kindness with firmness, humility with self-reliance, and an inquiring mind with an open mind." Dr. Slaughter concluded his message to the rapt crowd: "She served her day and generation by the will of God and has bequeathed to us a legacy of faithfulness, love, and devotion. May the mantle of her beautiful, useful life fall tenderly upon all who follow her Lord and Savior."

Tributes to WMU's remarkable leader continued to pour in, and time has not diminished the power of her influence. Kathleen Mallory had the gift of getting the best out of others. Women would frequently look back in amazement to discover all that God had done through their efforts, simply because their service was committed to Him. Even into this new millennium, there are still women living who directly recall the impact of Kathleen Mallory on their lives. Joyce (Mrs. John) Rogers, pastor's wife and longtime North Carolina WMU leader, vividly remembers meeting Miss Mallory in 1953 at the dedication of the Mallory Center in Baltimore. Joyce recalls, "Memories of the Kathleen Mallory Good Will Center are forever etched in my mind. My life was changed dramatically when the center was constructed in 1953, just two doors from my row house. And only five blocks away was the Lee Street Memorial Baptist Church. The missionaries who worked there were the first Christians I had ever met. I never knew the church was there until they visited me. No one in my family went to church." Joyce Rogers went on to explain the influence of the Mallory Center in her life and how she came to saving faith because of it. Every club that met at the center, she attended — even the Mother's Club! The center sent her to GA camp every summer, and she ended up being a counselor there. Through the life of this child, who was led to Christ by the efforts of Mallory Center, Joyce Rogers' entire family came to faith. It was just one year after the dedication of the center named for her that Kathleen Mallory went to her eternal reward. Nevertheless, her remarkable influence continues to be felt in countless places and in untold numbers.

Perhaps none of the much-deserved praise given to her reached the level of significance as did Kathleen Mallory's life of prayer. Her remarkable service literally grew out of prayer. One of Southern Baptist's greatest missions leaders, Dr. Baker James Cauthen, president of the Foreign Mission Board, summed it up in a personal remembrance. Dr. Cauthen was at a Southern Baptist Convention meeting, and, in order to meet an appointment, he entered the room in which the WMU executive committee was meeting. Just as he opened the door, Cauthen heard Miss Mallory say "Friends, God has granted us victory in letting us bring the largest Lottie Moon Christmas Offering we have ever had. Let us get down on our knees and thank Him and ask Him to bless its use in carrying the gospel to the uttermost parts of the earth." "Seeing the WMU on its knees in prayer is a blessing I shall never forget," Cauthen related. Before concluding, he said, "Necessary and welcome as the money is, the prayers mean more — far more."

Strong women dot the landscape of WMU's history along with Kathleen Mallory. There was the earliest influence of that extraordinary woman who was America's first missionary woman — Ann Hasseltine Judson. Judson, in turn, impacted a young woman in South Carolina, and Hephzibah Jenkins Townsend found a way to start a little society on Edisto Island in 1810 that eventually led to the formation of Woman's Missionary Union in 1888. Hephzibah's legacy extended to Annie Armstrong, WMU's first executive secretary, the woman whose force was so instrumental in shaping the constitution and framework of what became the world's largest missions organization for women. And there was the inimitable Fannie Exile Heck, WMU's great visionary, who left to generations that followed a peerless legacy in mission study, missions giving, children's organizations, their magazine, their prayer calendar — all of which remain thriving in the twenty-first century. And standing tall with them in this parade of hero hearts is the petite, quietly forceful, powerfully persuasive, awesomely self-disciplined, inspiring leader who served for close to four decades. Yet, above all, nothing so defined the character of Kathleen Moore Mallory as did prayer. Uniquely gifted — Kathleen Mallory was God's beautiful gift to Woman's Missionary Union.

APPENDIX

A new file has been discovered in the archives of Woman's Missionary Union, Birmingham, Alabama. It contains massive numbers of cards and letters from Kathleen Mallory to Fannie Heck, written *every day* during the fourteen months of her hospitalization for cancer. Mallory wrote small details of daily life in the WMU office, knowing of Miss Heck's love and concern for WMU and its purposes. They offer a poignant look into the deep friendship of the two national leaders of the organization. A sampling of those cards and letters is in this appendix. Especially moving is the letter Kathleen wrote Fannie on August 25, 1915. Fannie's last book, *Everyday Gladness,* was published and placed in Fannie's hands on August 23. A copy was mailed to Kathleen at the same time, and her August 25 letter is her response to Fannie's book. Mallory's letter was written on the day that Fannie died.

Also included in the appendix is a sampling of articles Kathleen Mallory sent from China in 1923-24 to be published in *Royal Service* and *World Comrades.* They give insight into Mallory's experiences in those months.

EDITORIAL

ORIENTATING

DICTIONARIES define the word orientate as a verb which means to turn toward the east, to veer from the north to the south toward the east. Orientating, therefore, means turning toward the east and explains what I am now doing for a period of eight months. Sailing from Seattle on August 31, I am due in Yokohama, Japan, on the 11th of September. The name of the good boat is the President McKinley of the Admiral Line, which holds the record of the quickest trips across the Pacific. My cabinmate is Miss Pearle Johnson returning to Shanghai and, as other traveling companions, I have the following missionary friends, most of whom are like me making their initial journey to the east:

Mr. and Mrs. M. O. Cheek	Miss Florence Jones
Lillimay Cheek (Age 7)	Miss Essie Smith
Miss Lillie Mae Hundley	Miss Nellie Lee Putney
Miss Lilla Echols	Miss Lora Clement
Miss Irene Jeffers	Mr. and Mrs. O. Gunnerfeldt
Miss Mary Helen Phillips	Miss Phebe Lawton
Miss Grace Wells	Miss Mary O. Walters
Miss Lucy Yao	Miss Florence Walne
Miss Lillian Thomason	Mr. and Mrs. A. Y. Napier
Miss Nell Darden Lawrence	Campbell Napier (Age 11)
Miss Winifred Moxon	Davis Napier (Age 8)
Mr. and Mrs. Harold Snuggs	Mr. E. M. Bostick
Mr. and Mrs. J. M. Rogers	Mr. W. W. Rankin
Edgar Rogers (Age 4)	Mr. and Mrs. D. W. Herring and Child
Miss Cynthia Miller	Mr. and Mrs. C. L. Culpepper and Baby
Miss Alice Huey	Dr. and Mrs. C. E. James and Baby

Misses Lawton, Walters and Walne will disembark with me in Japan, while all the others will proceed to China. Whether or not seasickness will incapacitate me for much social intercourse while on the boat, still I know that I will thoroughly enjoy the two weeks' companionship with these new and returning missionaries.

For five weeks I shall doubtless be in Japan, the Foreign Mission Board having kindly arranged for me to visit Yokohama, Tokyo, Nara, Kyoto, Kobe, Hiroshima, Kure, Shimonoseki, Kokura, Fukuoka, Kumamota and Nagasaki. One of the most delightful features of the Japanese trip will be the attendance upon the annual meeting of the Japanese W.M.U. Like most people I have from childhood longed to see Japan with its brilliant foliage and flowers, its vari-colored kimonas and its promising missions. I do hope that the maples will be all gold and red, the chrysanthemums in full bloom and the schools busy at their lessons. Beyond my fondest hope I know that I shall rejoice because of the visit to Japan.

From there I go to the North China Mission, visiting our workers and work at Tsingtao, Tsinan, Tsining, Taian, Pingtu, Laichow, Hwanghsien, Tengchow and Chefoo. Five weeks will thus be given to North China, the itinerary leading also to the historic city of Peking. Many have said that North China is our greatest missionary opportunity, so of course I shall be keenly interested while there, espe-

4

cially in the schools and hospitals and the evangelistic work which feeds them and is in turn fed by them. An added joy will be attendance upon the annual meeting of the North China W.M.U.

Early in December the schedule leads to the Interior China Mission with visits to Chengchow, Kaifeng, Pochow and Kweiteh. In Honan's rich province it will truly be a privilege to see how our work, at an advantage from its inception, is "going from strength to strength".

Nanking, Chinkiang, Yangchow and Wusih will all be visited before Christmas so that that sacred time may be spent in Shanghai, where our real Southern Baptist Convention work began over 75 years ago. There New Year's will also turn its leaf for me and perhaps until the middle of January I will remain there. Everyone says that Shanghai, the Paris of the east, is marvelous to behold and of course our excellent mission work there will afford many interesting opportunities. If possible, while in Shanghai I will write down my impressions of Japan and of the China already seen for if some good "muse" will help me I want to incorporate into book form the impressions of this orientating trip. To the memory of my father and mother, whose legacy is making the trip possible, I will dedicate the book if it seems at all worthy of their devoted interest in missions. In the book I shall also want to have many good pictures of our workers at their appointed tasks, the kodak for taking these pictures having been graciously given me by the W.M.U. Executive Committee.

From Shanghai a visit will be made to Soochow and then sailing via Manila I will go to Canton, the real birthplace of all our work in China. From there trips are planned to Shinchow, Shin Hing, Wuchow, Kong Moon, Sz Yap Field, Macao and Hong Kong. Practically the entire month of February will be spent in the South China Mission.

Just as our dear country is celebrating George Washington's birthday, my little U.S. flag and I will wave farewell to the orient and will "westward ho" take our course. Into the beautiful port of Honolulu we hope to sail and then before April 1st through the "Golden Gate" into San Francisco. The month of April will be used in work upon the aforesaid book and in seeing California and other western places. Certainly it will be a joy to journey then to Atlanta for the May annual meeting of the Woman's Missionary Union.

Thus in perhaps tedious detail I have outlined my plans for these orientating months. In my absence Miss Ethel Winfield will have charge of the Birmingham office, Miss Juliette Mather and Miss Blanche White will if possible increase their field work, Mrs. Maud R. McLure will attend at least four of the state annual meetings, Miss Willie Jean Stewart will prepare the outline programs for Home and Foreign Fields and the W.M.S. programs for the January and March Weeks of Prayer, while of course Mrs. James, fresh from her trip to the European missions, will lead as the Union's president. It is my purpose to write articles each month for ROYAL SERVICE, for Home and Foreign Fields and for the state denominational papers, with quarterly articles for WORLD COMRADES. Of course there will be much which can never be written in black and white but the wonderful field glasses, the gift of the Alabama W.M.U. Executive Committee, and I will do our very best to see as with your very own eyes. Pray that the report may be faithful as was Caleb's so that our W.M.U. women and young people may know henceforth that by their prayers and gifts of substance and self they are well able to possess Japan and China for Christ.—*Kathleen Mallory*

5

Alabama Baptist also ranks high in Christian work in Peking, namely, Mr. W. B. Pettus, who is head of the North China Language School. Seven southern Baptists are there this year trying to learn the language which will be their "point of contact" in approaching the Chinese. God grant that increasingly from year to year young men and women may thus learn how to "speak a good word for Jesus".

NU TSU WHEI OF NORTH CHINA

REVERED is the memory of Dr. J. B. Hartwell for his long devoted service in North China. He it was who chose as the title for the Woman's Missionary Union of North China the euphonious words, Nu Tsu Whei, the pronunciation being about as follows: "new zew whey", the exact translation of which is "woman's helpful association".

The second week in November its last annual session was held, the meeting place being Tsingtao, the Chinese city which was built by the Germans, beautified by the Japanese and returned to the Chinese by the Washington Conference. In keeping with the many excellent buildings in Tsingtao the Baptists have erected a two-story church building with many plans for institutional features. In this church the Nu Tsu Whei met for two days before the general association. Many of the delegates traveled for at least 60 miles of the journey in heavy wooden carts without the suggestion of a spring. They brought great bundles of quilts to serve as their bedding and slept in the Sunday school rooms of the church. To this meeting came also nine women missionaries, their number being increased by the resident missionaries, Mrs. Edgar Morgan and Mrs. Emmett Stephens. Throughout the meeting it was very evident that the Chinese women honor and really love their women missionaries. It was, however, equally apparent that they are very capable as presiding officers and as participants in the discussions from the floor. The president is Miss Jong, who teaches at Hwanghien. With characteristic Chinese reserve and yet with brightening eyes they listened to the treasurer's report, showing the year's apportionment for the campaign more than reached. They adopted II Cor. 5:5 as their year's watchword and also took Miss Heck's hymn as theirs for this new year. It certainly made our watchword and hymn have a new meaning for me and certainly I gave thanks for all those who have known that "He who wrought 'them for the redemption of China' is God". Very capably and yet modestly did Miss Jong present the woman's report to the general association, Miss Alice Huey introducing me so that I might give to that gathering even as I had previously done to the Nu Tsu Whei the greetings of our southern W.M.U.

The closing Sunday of the association was marked by a genuine spiritual fervor. Dr. Biederwolf, Mr. Rodeheaver and Miss Grace Saxe were present, being in Tsingtao by invitation from all the Christians of the city. On the bench with me there was a Swedish Baptist missionary, Miss Florence Lide of Hwanghien and a Chinese Christian woman. Back of me was a Japanese Christian woman. Truly it was inspiring as the great audience sang together in Chinese, Japanese and English, "Onward, Christian Soldiers". Fully thirty men and women took a definite stand for Christ, one being a Japanese.—*Kathleen Mallory*

Miss Mallory sent the words
back – we had them "pictured"

5

Temple Day in Pingtu

Dɪᴅ you count the crowd at the last ⛰ ? Of
course not and no more could I count the people who were
crowded closely together in the 🏯 and 🏯 yard
the Saturday I was in Pingtu in north China. About
2 X a year the people of that city and from the
really thousands of nearby villages come together to
celebrate what is called " 🏯 Day." All the 🚪
of the temple yard and of the many buildings are swung
wide 🚪 🚪 and the people swarm within. The day we
were there, many of them had brought all kinds of things
to sell, such as peanuts, persimmons, cooked meat, fur
caps and what not, but the one thing almost everybody
seemed to be buying was imitation paper money. It was
yellow, about a 👣 square and had on it the imprint
of a Chinese dollar. One woman told us that she had
that morning bought fifty cents worth of such paper and
I feel sure that many if not most of the people had
bought more for she looked quite poor. And what did they
do with the paper? Why they threw it into a great stone

6   WORLD COMRADES

fire close by the temple! Why did they waste it

this way? Because their heathen religion had taught
them to believe that by doing so they would make it
possible for their loved ones, who were already dead,
to have that much money to spend in the spirit world!

Up in the chief 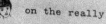 building we saw many people

lighting incense sticks in front of a very ugly big

wooden 🗿 which they called the "City God". While they

were kow-towing or knocking their 👤 on the really

dirty floor before him, the priest was striking a 🔔

and another man was beating a huge , while great

trays of food were being presented to the wooden "god"
for his blessing, though "selfishly" only a very small
portion of each thing was left for him to "eat".

And what do you suppose happened to that " 🗿 " that

afternoon? Why he was put into a big sedan 🪑 , all

covered with red, and by poles over men's shoulders he

was taken to another to visit his wife's mother!

In front of his chair went many men who did not really
look like men for they had on big and very ugly wooden

masks to represent  ,  and

the like. Then there followed two huge red Chinese

 with any number of small strips of cloth

sewed on them. We were told that in all there were
20,000 strips, each bearing the name of a person who
had that morning paid the priest to pray for them!

--Kathleen Mallory

Six Leaders of Comrades in W. M. U. Work

L	J	F	I	W
L	A	N	I	S
T	O	M	E	L
R	H	W	R	D
A	Y	E	N	

Move from square to square in any direction.

Ella B. Robertson

Woman's Missionary Union

Auxiliary to Southern Baptist Convention

15 W. Franklin Street, Baltimore, Md.

Baltimore, Maryland.   October 8, 1914.

Miss Fannie E.S.Heck,
c/o Hygeia Hospital,
Richmond, Va.

Dear Miss Heck:

My dear friend, May Keller, will come up
from Richmond on Friday night and you know with what
pleasure I am awaiting her. It seems now that I shall
have all of the January programs finished by that time
and I feel sure that we can be together a great deal.
She is thoroughly enjoying her work at Westhampton
College. The school opened with 100 students.

I wish that you could have seen an enormous
steel frame which passed up Cathedral Street this
morning. It took ten horses to pull the wagon. I do
not know what missionary talk I can get out of it but
it was very impressive and quite systematic.

Yours lovingly,

KM/CEH

Kathleen Mallory.

My dear Miss Heck   Thursday

Woman's Missionary Union, Southern Baptist Conv., 15 W. Franklin St., Balto., Md.

A lady has just been in who knows where
the old minutes kept by Mrs. Graves in 1872 are and
she is going to let us copy them. It will be interesting
to have this interdenominational information on file.
Mr. Myers of the Missionary Education Movement
came in this morning on his way from a missionary conference in Richmond and I have promised
if possible to lead another class at Blue Ridge next
June. I want after that to go on to Ridge Crest. Mollie
sent me today some of her delicious birthday cake and
some pecans from our own home yard. My, but we are
enjoying them and I only wish I could share them with
you. Could you possibly eat them? Lovingly, K. Mallory.

Woman's Missionary Union, Southern Baptist Conv., 15 W. Franklin St., Balto., Md.

My dear Miss Heck: Thursday:

This afternoon, Jesse, the janitor, has planted
another crop of oats in the window boxes. This makes
three crops so far. They last only about two weeks
but oh they do look so pretty and green. The poin-
settia which the girls gave me last Christmas is in
splendid condition and should bloom beautifully
this winter. That time seems afar off for it is very
hot today. Really last night was uncomfortable.
When Mary, Keith and I got out from prayer meeting
we went to an ice-cream parlor so you know we
were desperate!! She seems quite busy here at the
Hopkins. With loving greetings from all — Kathleen Mallory

Woman's Missionary Union, Southern Baptist Conv., 15 W. Franklin St., Balto., Md.

My dear Miss Heck: Friday.

Last night I sewed to my heart's content. There is hardly anything which I would rather do than to mend or alter things and last night I fixed a dress and a waist — my dark blue satin dress and white satin waist. These will fill in a good deal this winter. Today all of the week of Prayer literature was mailed or expressed. I am so thankful. Dr. Willingham and Dr. Smith have both written in approval. The proof In December Royal Service is in and Mrs. _____ and I will get to proof-reading. Loving greetings to Your mother. I do hope you have had a good day.

                                    most lovingly,
                                    K. Mallory.

Woman's Missionary Union, Southern Baptist Conv., 15 W. Franklin St., Balto., Md.

                                    November 24,1914.

    Dear Miss Heck:
                    This afternoon, I am to tell a
    Thanksgiving story to the little German children
    at our Locust Point settlement. I spent the
    morning over at the Pratt Library trying to find
    some interesting Thanksgiving story. I got one
    which I hope will be worth while. It was almost
    like finding a needle in a haystack.
            It is a beautiful day here and I do hope
    it is so with you.

                    Yours lovingly,

                    Kathleen Mallory

Woman's Missionary Union, Southern Baptist Conv., 15 W. Franklin St., Balto., MD.

December 19, 1914.

Dear Miss Heck:

Yesterday I spent practically
all the time getting my materials ready for
ROYAL SERVICE. I have finished everything
except one page of the editorial department. I
am still turning over in my mind the thoughts
about George Washington for that editorial
but the hatchet story is so prominent that
I do not seem to be able to cut my way further.
Hoping to win out yet,
I am,
Yours lovingly,

Kathleen Mallory

Woman's Missionary Union, Southern Baptist Conv., 15 W. Franklin St., Balto., MD.

December 22, 1914.

Dear Miss Heck:

Your letter came yesterday
and I cannot tell you how happy it has made us.
There seems to be a new light in our sky and
we are so thankful that you can say that
you are feeling better. Our Christmas wreaths
are up at the windows and this morning Miss
Claris Crane brought us some beautiful evergreens. I wish that we could share them
with you.
Yours lovingly,

Kathleen Mallory

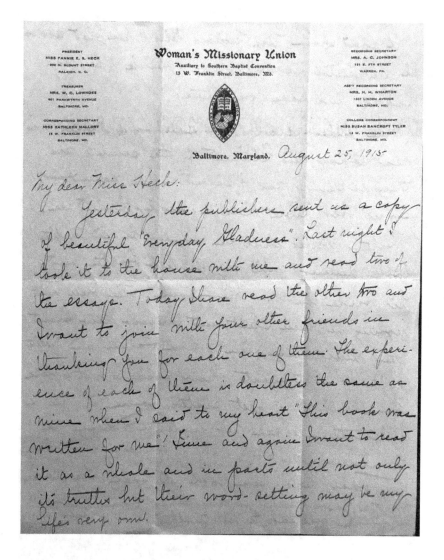

Woman's Missionary Union
Auxiliary to Southern Baptist Convention
15 W. Franklin Street, Baltimore, Md.

PRESIDENT
MISS FANNIE E. S. HECK
200 N. BLOUNT STREET
RALEIGH, N. C.

TREASURER
MRS. W. C. LOWNDES
601 PARKWYRTH AVENUE
BALTIMORE, MD.

CORRESPONDING SECRETARY
MISS KATHLEEN MALLORY
15 W. FRANKLIN STREET
BALTIMORE, MD.

RECORDING SECRETARY
MRS. A. C. JOHNSON
101 E. 5TH STREET
WARREN, PA.

ASS'T RECORDING SECRETARY
MRS. H. M. WHARTON
1502 LINDEN AVENUE
BALTIMORE, MD.

COLLEGE CORRESPONDENT
MISS SUSAN BANCROFT TYLER
15 W. FRANKLIN STREET
BALTIMORE, MD.

Baltimore, Maryland, August 25, 1915

My dear Miss Heck:

Yesterday, the publishers sent us a copy of beautiful "Everyday Gladness". Last night I took it to the house with me and read two of the essays. Today I have read the other two and I want to join with your other friends in thanking you for each one of them. The experience of each of them is doubtless the same as mine when I said to my heart "This book was written for me"! Time and again I want to read it as a whole and in parts until not only its truths but their word-setting may be my life's very own.

A card from Mrs. Simms tells of her glad arrival in Clifton Springs. I love to think of her as happy and care-free there.

The galley-proof of the Calendar of Prayer was read today and returned to the printer. Mrs. Dill certainly has prepared a fine calendar for us. Her Bible readings fairly thrilled me.

Father writes that on Sunday he and Mother took dinner with my younger brother and his bride in their new home. They were just moving in when I left and I know how proud they must have been to have Father and Mother as their first guests. Their home is just across from our youngest sister's home. It will be interesting to see her instruct them in housekeeping. Mrs Byars Sunbeam leader for Texas, sends love to you.

Today has been cool and fair. The flowers in the yard seem so grateful. Lovingly, Aug 23 1905. Loving greetings to your mother. Kathleen Mallory

Chapter Sources

Preface

Ussery, Annie Wright, *The Story of Kathleen Mallory.* (Nashville, Tennessee: Broadman Press, 1956), 194-196.

Hunt, Alma, *History of Woman's Missionary Union.* (Nashville, Tennessee: Convention Press, 1964), 95.

Hunt, Rosalie Hall, *We've a Story to Tell: 125 Years of WMU.* (Birmingham, Alabama: WMU, 2014), 364-366.

Chapter One

Ussery, Annie Wright, *The Story of Kathleen Mallory.* (Nashville, Tennessee: Broadman Press, 1956), 1-7.

Allen, Catherine, *Laborers Together With God.* (Birmingham, Alabama: Woman's Missionary Union, 1987), 182.

Mallory Family Bible

Chapter Two

Ussery, Annie Wright, *The Kathleen Mallory Story,* 1-8.

Allen, Catherine, *Laborers Together with God,* 182-183.

Chapter Three

Jackson, Walter, *Our Time in History, 1842-1942: First Baptist Church, Selma.* (Selma, Alabama: Clairmont Press, 1992), 175.

Mallory Family Bible

Ussery, 1-9.

Allen, *Laborers,* 182-183.

Chapter Four
Ussery, 8-13.
Johns Hopkins Catalogue, 1901-1902.

Chapter Five
Ussery, 11-20.
Mallory Bible

Chapter Six
Ussery, 13-20.
WMU Archives

Chapter Seven
Ussery, 25-32, 33-37.
The Alabama Baptist, October 6, 1908.
Hunt, R. *We've a Story to Tell: 125 Years of WMU.* (Birmingham, Alabama: Woman's Missionary Union, 2014), 363-364.

Chapter Eight
Allen, *Laborers,* 184-185.
Hunt, R. *We've a Story,* 126-127.
Ussery, 34-39.
Southern Baptist Historical Library and Archives, letter, James Frost to Kathleen Mallory, January 6, 1910.

Chapter Nine
Allen, *Laborers,* 184-185.
Cox, 76-77.

WMU Archives, Letter, Kathleen Mallory to Alma Hunt, December 30, 1940.

Hunt, Rosalie Hall, *Out of Exile: Fannie Heck and the Rest of the Story.* (Greenville, South Carolina, Courier Publishing), 265-269.

Foreign Mission Board, Southern Baptist Convention. Kathleen Mallory to R. T. Willingham, September 5, 1912, James Frost to Kathleen Mallory, February 19, 1915.

Chapter Ten

Hunt, R. *We've a Story,* 128-131.

Cox, 83-85.

Ussery, 42-49.

Hunt, R. *Exile,* 269-271.

SBHLA, Letter, Kathleen Mallory to Dr. James Frost, February 17, 1915.

SBHLA, Telegram, Frost letters.

Chapter Eleven

Allen, *Century to Celebrate,* 124, 306, 323, 347, 354.

SBHLA: Letter, Dr. James Frost to Kathleen Mallory, February 17, 1915.

WMU Archives: Mallory papers, Southern Baptist Theological Seminary, Interview with Duke McCall.

SBHLA: Letter, Mallory to Dr. Van Ness, December 16, 1975.

Mallory to Van Ness, June 17, June 18, 1926.

Allen, *Laborers,* 185-187.

Ussery, 50.

Hunt, R. *We've a Story,* 135.

Hunt, A. *History of Woman's Missionary Union,* 97.

Chapter Twelve

Allen, *Century to Celebrate,* 206, 259.

Hunt, R. *We've a Story,* 135-137.

Ussery, 51-52, 56-58, 60.

Hunt, A. 95, 99, 101-103, 107.

Mallory Family Bible

Cox, 84-87.

Chapter Thirteen

Allen, *Century to Celebrate,* 60, 125-130, 308.

Hunt, R. *We've a Story,* 135-137.

Hunt, A. 104-106.

Allen, *Laborers,* 188.

Ussery, 55-63.

Chapter Fourteen

Allen, *Century,* 63-65, 182, 204.

Allen, *Laborers,* 287-289.

Royal Service, April, 1916.

Annual Report, WMU, 1920.

Hunt, R. *We've a Story,* 139, 222-223, 335-336.

Hunt, A. 111-114.

Ussery, 62.

WMU Archives, Letter, Mary Rawlins, *Florida Times Union,*
    May 20, 1921.

Chapter Fifteen

Hunt, R. *We've a Story,* 141-142.

Allen, *Century to Celebrate,* 132-133.

Ussery, 64-65.

Flynt, J. Wayne and Gerald W. Berkley. *Taking Christianity to China: Alabama Missionaries in the Middle Kingdom, 1850-1950.* (Tuscaloosa: University of Alabama Press, 1997,) 146, 156, 351.

[Author's note: Grace Wells, my mother's oldest sister, who lived next door to us in Chinkiang (Zhenjiang) in the 1940s, was one of the new missionaries headed to China in 1923 who shared the voyage with Kathleen Mallory.]

Chapter Sixteen

Hunt, R. *We've a Story,* 142, 146-147.

Ussery, 84-87, 93-94, 119-122.

Allen, *Century to Celebrate,* 134-135.

Cox, 90-91.

SBHLA, Letter, Kathleen Mallory to Una Roberts Lawrence, March 30, 1926, April 30, 1926.

Chapter Seventeen

Hunt, A. 117-129, 134-135.

Ussery, 96-98.

Allen, *Century to Celebrate,* 130-131, 137, 143, 149-151, 156.

Hunt, R. *We've a Story,* 146-151.

Allen, *Laborers,* 71-72, 186.

WMU Archives: Interview with Martha Morgan, who worked

with Ethlene Boone Cox her last 19 years.

[Author's family records. Author's mother, Alice Wells Hall, was one of the eight missionaries who sailed to China on the *SS Empress of Asia* in 1929, all of whom had their salaries funded by WMU.]

Chapter Eighteen

Allen, *Century to Celebrate.* 241-249.

Hunt, R. *We've a Story,* 153-154, 346-347.

Ussery, 109-110, 119-122.

Hunt, A. 100, 144-145.

Cox, 93.

WMU Archives: Personal reflections of France Tyler.

Allen, *Laborers,* 71-76, 79, 188.

Chapter Nineteen

Ussery, 135-136, 151-153.

Allen, *Century to Celebrate,* 241-251.

Washington, Sondra. *The Story of Nannie Helen Burroughs.*
    (Birmingham, Alabama: WMU, 2006,) 122.

SBHLA: Nannie Helen Burroughs papers, Letter, Kathleen
    Mallory to Nannie Helen Burroughs, September 1936.

Allen, *Laborers,* 189.

Hunt, A. 145-149.

Hunt, R. *We've a Story,* 148, 159-160.

Baptist and Reflector, Tennessee Baptist Convention, August 10,
    1939, No. 32.

[Author's note: Moonbeam Tong, who represented China

at the 1938 Jubilee annual meeting of WMU, was an English student of the author's mother's at the University of Shanghai. She requested her teacher's help in choosing an English name. Her given name in Chinese meant "the light of the moon," so she proposed that her English version be: "Moonshine." Alice Wells, her instructor, gently encouraged her to make it "Moonbeam," and that is the name she chose.]

Chapter Twenty

Hunt, R. *We've a Story,* 160, 164-165.

Ussery, 152-154.

Allen, *Century to Celebrate,* 132, 158, 249-257, 261.

Royal Service. April 1943, January 1944, May 1943.

SBHLA: Correspondence, Kathleen Mallory and Nannie Helen Burroughs, April 13, 1940, May 27, 1940, July 15, July 19, July 20, August 13, 1940.

[Author's note: A number of years ago, a volunteer's personal recollections of working with Kathleen Mallory were related to Angie Cooper of Tuscaloosa, Al, a longtime admirer of the life and ministry of Miss Mallory.]

Chapter Twenty-One

SBHLA: Letter, Kathleen Mallory to W.O Carver, July 23, 1945, February 21, 1948.

Ussery, 158, 160-166.

Allen, *Laborers,* 190.

Hunt, A. 154-157.

Hunt, R. *We've a Story,* 168-171.

Chapter Twenty-Two

Hunt, R. *We've a Story,* 173-175.

Ussery, 160-188.

Hunt, A. 156, 165.

Chapter Twenty-Three

Ussery, 188-199.

Epilogue

Annual Report Minutes, 1955. Presenting Miss Kathleen
  Mallory, 1912-1948.

Ussery, 197-199.

WMU Archives: "Recollections of Miss Mallory," by Rose Pye
  (Arkansas).

Quarterly Review, July-August-September, 1948, 11-15.

BIBLIOGRAPHY

Allen, Catherine, *A Century to Celebrate*. Birmingham, Alabama: Woman's Missionary Union (WMU), 1987.

_____, *Laborers Together with God*. Birmingham, Alabama: WMU, 1987.

Burroughs, Nannie Helen. Correspondence of Burroughs with Una Roberts Lawrence and Kathleen Mallory. Nashville, Tennessee: Southern Baptist Historical Library and Archives.

Carver, Dr. W.O. Correspondence of Carver with Kathleen Mallory. Nashville, Tennessee: Southern Baptist Historical Library and Archives.

Cox, Ethlene Boone, *Following in His Train*. Nashville, Tennessee: Broadman Press, 1938.

_____. Ethlene Boone papers. Birmingham, Alabama: WMU archives.

Flynt, J. Wayne and Gerald W. Berkley. *Taking Christianity to China: Alabama Missionaries in the Middle Kingdom, 1850-1950*. Tuscaloosa, Alabama: University of Alabama Press, 1997.

Frost, Dr. James. Correspondence with Kathleen Mallory and

others. Nashville, Tennessee: Southern Baptist Historical Library and Archives.

Heck, Fannie Exile Scudder, *In Royal Service*. Richmond, Virginia: Foreign Mission Board, SBC, 1913.

Hunt, Alma, *History of Woman's Missionary Union*. Nashville, Tennessee: Convention Press, 1964.

Hunt, Rosalie Hall, *Bless God and Take Courage*. Valley Forge, Pennsylvania: Judson Press, 2005.

_____. *Her Way: The Remarkable Story of Hephzibah Jenkins Townsend*. Greenville, South Carolina: Courier Publishing, 2016.

_____. *A Life Beyond Boundaries: The Extraordinary Story of Ann Hasseltine Judson*. Valley Forge, Pennsylvania: Judson Press, 2017.

_____. *Out of Exile: Fannie Heck and the Rest of the Story*. Greenville, South Carolina: Courier Publishing, 2019.

_____. *We've a Story to Tell: 125 Years of WMU*. Birmingham, Alabama: WMU, 2014.

Jackson, Walter. *Our Time in History: 1842-1942, First Baptist Church, Selma*. Selma: Clairmont Press, 1992.

Jackson, Hermione and Mary Essie Stephens. *Women of Vision: History of Woman's Missionary Union of Alabama.* Montgomery, Alabama: Woman's Missionary Union of Alabama, 1988.

Lawrence, Una Roberts. Correspondence of Lawrence with Kathleen Mallory and Nannie Helen Burroughs. Nashville, Tennessee: Southern Baptist Historical Library and Archives.

Mallory Family Bible. Selma, Alabama: First Baptist Church, Kathleen Mallory Memorial Parlor.

Mallory, Kathleen Moore. Correspondence of Mallory with key Southern Baptist leaders. Nashville, Tennessee: Southern Baptist Historical Library and Archives.

_____. Mallory papers and files. Birmingham, Alabama: National WMU Archives.

Pye, Lila Westbrook. *The Yield of the Golden Years: A History of the Baptist Woman's Missionary Union of Arkansas, Written to Commemorate the Golden Jubilee.* Privately published, 1938.

Ussery, Annie Wright. *The Story of Kathleen Mallory.* Nashville, Tennessee: Broadman Press, 1956.

Washington, Sondra. *The Story of Nannie Helen Burroughs.* Birmingham, Alabama: WMU, 2006.